Corolla V...
Walking Tour Map

D0558911

E Corolla Light Town Center

Map Artwork by Gary Crane

Recreation   Restaurant   Shopping   Accommodation

Corolla

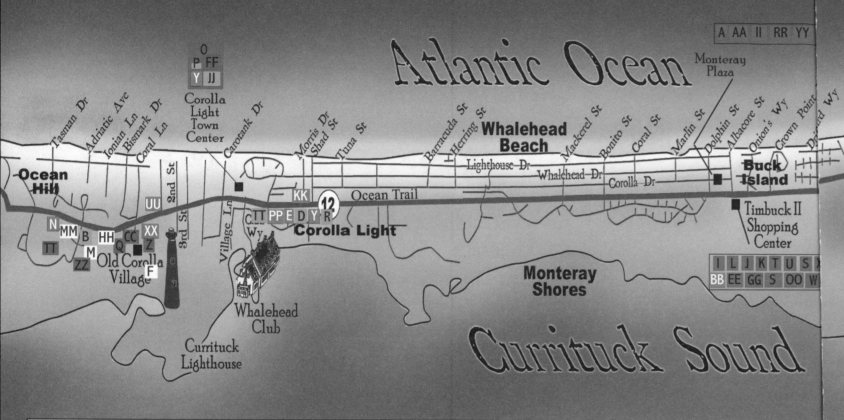

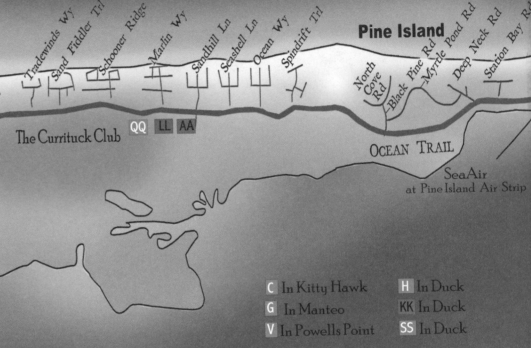

Atlantic Ocean

Pine Island

Monteray Plaza

A AA II RR YY

Whalehead Beach

Buck Island

The Currituck Club   QQ LL AA

OCEAN TRAIL

Ocean Trail

Timbuck II Shopping Center

SeaAir at Pine Island Air Strip

Ocean Hill

Corolla Light Town Center

Corolla Light

I L J K T U S X
BB EE GG S OO W

Monteray Shores

Old Corolla Village

Whalehead Club

Currituck Lighthouse

Currituck Sound

C In Kitty Hawk   **H** In Duck
G In Manteo   **KK** In Duck
V In Powells Point   **SS** In Duck

Index of Sponsors Located in Corolla—

Recreation   **Restaurant**   **Shopping**   **Accommodation**

Corolla

Walking Tour & Guide Book

Fourth Edition

Corolla

Walking Tour & Guide Book

By Norris Austin, Molly Harrison & Lee Schindel

Published by Narayana, Inc.
DBA One Boat Guides,
Michael McOwen, Publisher
P.O. Box 308 • Manteo, NC 27954

(252) 202-5548
e-mail: Michael@OneBoatGuides.com
4th Edition
1st Printing

ISBN 0-9768164-5-8

TABLE OF CONTENTS

ACKNOWLEDGMENTS

ringing this book to life required the combined efforts of many people. So many thank yous and acknowledgments are due that it's hard to know where to begin.

For this edition we are so thrilled to have a whole section of stories and photographs from Corolla native Norris Austin. The stories are in Norris' words and they add a rich new dimension to the book. We are so glad that Norris decided to publish them here. Norris has been a supporter of this guide from the beginning. In the writing of the Walking Tour, Norris endured countless interviews, last-minute phone calls, draft reviews and general brain-picking beyond the call of duty.

Thanks to Corolla former resident Shirley Austin for taking the time to sit down with me and share a few stories and memories about Corolla, and to Jewell Scarborough for doing the same (plus adding in a few Christmas cookies, books and photographs as well). Thanks to Hope Beacham and Bea Berle for the time they spent in the summer of 2002 telling me stories of Corolla and the northern beaches. Special thanks to Ed Lawler for sharing his 1970s memories and photos of Corolla.

Sharon Twiddy was a great asset to this guide, helping to get us started, taking us on a tour, checking in once in a while, finding facts and tracking down people, offering photographs and reviewing manuscripts.

Penne Smith-Sandbeck was so kind to offer her research material for the Architectural Survey of the Corolla and Currituck Banks area. All of the references to architectural styles in this guide are the result of Penne's diligent research and generosity.

Edna Baden at The Whalehead Club was an enthusiastic supporter of this guide. Thanks, Edna, for all of your interest, editorial assistance, the many private Whalehead Club tours — and for sharing the Whalehead Club's amazing stockpile of photographs.

Everyone at Outer Banks Conservationists and the Currituck Beach Lighthouse was especially helpful. Thanks to past executive director Lloyd Childers, who encouraged us to do this book from the start and gave us so much information and assistance. Thanks also to Bill Parker, John Wilson and everyone else at OBC who helped us out.

A great many thanks to Lee Schindel, who tackled the updating of the guidebook, an enormous feat, with competence and grace. Thanks to all the business owners in Corolla who were so willing to help her get all the details right for the guidebook section.

Attention and mention should be showered upon Gary Crane for creating the Corolla map, and Beth Storie for her eyeballing and editorial expertise. Also to Nealy Butler for the great work on ad production.

MH & MM

INTRODUCTION

Welcome to Corolla on the glorious Outer Banks of North Carolina! The name Corolla means different things to different people. For natives and longtime Outer Bankers, the name brings to mind the tiny village that once thrived near Currituck Beach Lighthouse. For visitors and newcomers, Corolla is a seaside resort area stretched out along the entire Currituck Outer Banks. Corolla then and Corolla now. As you'll see in this book, these are two very different places.

The first part of the book takes you through the history of old Corolla Village. We are so thrilled that this edition includes a new section featuring the stories, memories and photographs of longtime Corolla resident Norris Austin. This is Corolla history first-hand, and its very entertaining reading. The second part guides you along the Corolla Village Walking Tour, a specially mapped out and well-planned tour from the Whalehead Club and Currituck Beach Lighthouse to the historic homes and buildings of Corolla Village. Before reading Norris's stories and taking the Walking Tour, you will probably find it helpful to read the short history of Corolla and the Currituck Outer Banks that follows.

The third part of the book, the Corolla Guide, gives you the inside scoop on the attractions, activities, shops, restaurants and places to stay in this area of the Outer Banks. Whether you're planning a visit or are already here and looking for something to do, you'll find what you need in this guide.

Overview of Corolla

One of the first things you'll notice about Corolla is that it's new. Less than twenty years ago, Corolla was one of the last beach frontiers on the East Coast, with miles of empty land and only a few vacation homes dotting the dunes. Until 1984, the area was blocked off to everyone but a few landowners, but when the gates opened, a flood of development followed.

With expansive Atlantic beaches, luxurious seaside accommodations, polished landscaping and upscale shopping and dining complexes, Corolla is an increasingly popular East Coast vacation destination. It is a world of contemporary luxuries, where vacationing is easy and life is civilized.

Corolla sprung up so fast and its architecture is so new-fashioned that few people realize Corolla actually has deep roots dating back to the 1800s. Few people realize that Corolla was originally the name for a small village that sits beneath the

Corolla in the 1940s.

Currituck Beach Lighthouse. It has only been in recent years that people starting using the term Corolla to refer to the whole stretch of northern Outer Banks from the Dare County line to the end of the paved road.

This new Corolla is really the Currituck Outer Banks. In this stretch of Currituck County there are no incorporated towns; rather, there are numerous named subdivisions or planned developments — Pine Island, the Currituck Club, Ocean Sands, Whalehead, Buck Island, Monteray Shores, Corolla Light, Villages at Ocean Hill and others. Corolla is just a descriptive moniker, the name of the post office, not an official town designation. Since there are so many different subdivision names and everyone gets their mail through the Corolla Post Office, it is easiest to call everything on the Currituck Outer Banks "Corolla."

Surrounded by the Currituck Sound and Atlantic Ocean, the Currituck Outer Banks seems like a barrier island, but it is actually a barrier spit, or peninsula. The long, narrow spit of land is attached to the state of Virginia on the northern end and continues all the way down through Duck, Kitty Hawk, Kill Devil Hills and Nags Head to Oregon Inlet, where the ocean rushes through to meet the sound.

By the way, on the Outer Banks we pronounce Corolla as "Cor-AH-lah." Those who say "Cor-OLL-ah," as in the car made by Toyota, are immediately pegged as tourists.

The newness of Corolla can be refreshing. Nothing is rundown. Everything is clean. All of the buildings are air-conditioned. There are no potholes in the paved roads. The developments are well planned, not haphazard. But the lack of apparent roots can be unsettling. You might find yourself craving the sight of a few old houses. You might find yourself digging your toes deep into the sand, searching for the lineage of the land. Don't worry. Corolla does have heritage. You just have to look a little harder to find the history that's overshadowed in this vacation boomtown.

The history of the area is in what's left of old Corolla Village, the hunt club culture and in the memories of the few true natives who still live here. The quiet village roads, the turn-of-the-(last)-century houses, the Currituck Beach Lighthouse and The Whalehead Club speak volumes of stories about the long-gone days of the true Corolla old Corolla Village.

HISTORY OF COROLLA VILLAGE AND THE CURRITUCK OUTER BANKS 🐎

The place names of this area reflect the early Native American heritage. Currituck is a derivation of a Native American word meaning "land of the wild goose." Chowanog, Poteskeet, Pamunkey and other tribes that lived on the mainland used the barrier island as fishing and hunting grounds and named it for its abundance of geese. Europeans, who began settling in the area in the 1600s, applied the word to the barrier island, the county, the sound and two inlets.

In the late 1600s and early 1700s, a few European settlers resided on the northern barrier islands, but most people preferred to live on the mainland. Until the early 1800s, Currituck Banks was separated from Virginia by Old and New Currituck inlets and from Duck by Caffeys Inlet, so getting there was only possible by boat.

By the mid-1800s there were several communities, tiny hamlets really, dotting the northern Outer Banks. There was Wash Woods nearest to the Virginia line, Seagull a little farther down near Penny's Hill, Jones's Hill, a.k.a. Whaleshead or Currituck Beach (now Corolla), and Poyners Hill between Corolla and Duck. The communities were extremely isolated and

Bamber Photo Courtesy: Outer Banks Conservationists

The dock at the Currituck Beach Light Station in the 1890s.

remote, set amidst the untamed marshes and dunes of the banks.

The early residents of the banks fished and hunted to make a modest living. There were even reports of whalers here. They tended gardens and raised livestock, which ran at large on the barrier island. The bankers patrolled the beach to salvage items that washed ashore from numerous shipwrecks, and they recycled many of their goods in creative ways because supplies were hard to get. They traveled by boat to the mainland to sell waterfowl or fish, to purchase supplies or to visit friends and family. The locals also found work guiding and helping wealthy sportsmen from the north who hunted on the Currituck Sound.

In 1892, a writer from Harpers Weekly wrote about the Currituck Banks, "If there were any spot on earth that one would expect to find untenanted, it surely would be this stretch of sand between ocean and sound. ... Yet there is a hardy race who

have lived here from father to son for over a century. They exist entirely by hunting, fishing, rearing cattle and acting as guides."

Of these villages, the only one that stood the test of time was Corolla. Other villages petered out as times got hard, but a few residents always hung in there at Corolla. The village was able to thrive partly because of its abundance of government jobs, which offered steady pay. In 1873, when the village was still known as Jones's Hill, construction began on the Currituck Beach Lighthouse. The red-brick lighthouse, which towered over the small village and the banks, was completed and lit on December 1, 1875. The light keepers and their families added several new residents to the village.

In 1874 the U.S. Life Saving Service established the Jones's Hill Life Saving Station just east of the Currituck Beach Lighthouse site. This station, which was moved south and later known as Currituck Beach Life Saving Station, was one of the seven original life-saving stations on the Outer Banks. Seven local men were hired to staff the station from December through March. The keeper in charge received a salary of $200 a year, while the six surfmen were paid $40 a month for four months, with an additional $3 for every wreck they attended. The surfmen lived at the station, while their families resided in the village.

By 1895 Jones's Hill was busy enough to have its own post office. The postal service, notorious for changing the traditional names of Outer Banks villages, required that the villagers send in several suggestions for an official name. The story goes that they submitted Jones's Hill and Currituck Beach and were looking for other suggestions when someone mentioned that the inner part of a flower is called a corolla. That name was submitted and chosen by the postal service, forever changing the name of the small village. Norris Austin tells this story in his collection of stories in this book.

Corolla's population was large enough to require a church and schoolhouse. The children of the village had been attending various small schools, but in 1905 Currituck County was ready to support the one-room local school. The county provided a teacher, schoolbooks and standardized grading, and all the children of all grades attended the school together.

In 1922 another work opportunity arrived in the village when Edward and Marie-Louise LeBel Knight began work on Corolla Island (now the Whalehead Club). When the massive house on the sound was finally was finished in 1925, it must have been quite a sight to the modest-living locals. The residence provided many work opportunities for the locals. The Knights

employed local men as caretakers and hunting guides to accompany their invited guests.

In the 1930s it is said that more than 100 people lived at the village of Corolla. The Depression hit hard in the rest of the country, but on the banks people were able to survive off the wealth of the land and sea. During the period after the Depression, CCC and WPA boys were hired all along the Outer Banks to construct the high dunes and plant stabilizing grasses along the oceanfront and to improve the roads in the villages.

World War II had a strong impact on the village of Corolla. The U.S. Coast Guard leased the Corolla Island clubhouse to use as a training base, bringing hundreds of sailors-in-training to the village. German U-boats came close to the shoreline of the Outer Banks, and locals were required to darken their windows and use no headlights when driving on the beach. The village bustled with the influx of servicemen; the church services were full and the post office and store were always busy.

After the war, the population of Corolla dwindled rapidly. Many residents left the banks to look for jobs on the mainland. The lighthouse, electrified in 1939, no longer required several keepers, just a caretaker. (The villagers, however, didn't get electricity until 1955.) In the late 1950s Corolla's population reached its lowest point. The school closed for lack of students, and there were only a few families residing in the village. The church sat empty. The Whalehead Club was empty most of the year, though it was used as a boys' school, Corolla Academy, in the summers. Later The Whalehead Club was converted into the headquarters

Goose pond with decoys in front of the Currituck Beach Life Saving Station.

for Atlantic Research, a rocket-fuel testing facility.

In the 1970s only about 15 people lived in the village. People who visited or lived there back then say that Corolla felt like the absolute end of the earth. The road leading to Corolla was just a clay trail along the soundside, with "truck-swallowing holes" and sugar-fine sand that was nearly impossible to drive through. The Whalehead Club and lighthouse buildings were in grave disrepair. Corolla was wild and rugged. It was the last coastal getaway of the grandest kind, and anyone who ever went there fell in love with it just exactly like it was.

By the 1970s alternative vacationers were beginning to discover the isolated beaches of the Currituck Banks. Since there were no paved roads leading into Corolla, people drove on the beach from Virginia or Duck. But in 1974, U.S. Fish and Wildlife blocked the Virginia border to prevent excessive traffic in its Back Bay National Wildlife Refuge. Corolla residents were given special passes to be able to go through the gate. The border is still closed today.

Meanwhile, developers were buying up sizeable chunks of the Currituck Outer Banks. Ocean Sands and Whalehead were the first large-scale developments on the banks north of Duck. To keep people out of the private developments, the developers constructed a guard gate at the south end of the road leading up the banks. The guard was not allowed to let anyone but property owners past the gate. Sightseers were turned away, but many of them drove up on the beach anyway.

The southern guard gate didn't come down until October 1984, when the state took over the road and made it part of N.C. Highway 12. The state extended the road to pass through Corolla, and it was the village's first paved road. With the road open, interest in real estate jumped immediately, and the rest of the Currituck Banks story is quite apparent today.

Development came quickly. Former residents say the change was cataclysmic. Over the next decade, more than 1,500 homes were built on the Currituck Banks between the Dare County line and Corolla village. (In 1984 there were 422 homes, but by 1995 there were 1,966 homes.) By the year 2000, there were 2,750 homes in that same area. Almost all of these homes are second homes and vacation rentals, sitting empty for most of the year. More then 50 percent of the homes are greater than 5,000 square feet.

All this development quickly filled the empty land on the Currituck Banks, the land that used to provide a nest of isolation to Corolla village. Miraculously, the tiny core of the village has managed to maintain its boundaries and to keep typical Outer Banks development out, though it is a much different place today than it used to be. Many of the historic buildings have been adapted to modern uses, but their character and the sense of village is still intact.

But don't mistake what you see today for what Corolla village used to be. Many of the buildings you see today are new construction or have been moved to the village from other places. Down the road, the Currituck Beach Lighthouse and The Whalehead Club have developed modern appeal as tourist attractions. Even so, these attractions and old Corolla village buildings stand in marked contrast to the modern development of the Currituck Outer Banks, helping us to remember that Corolla does indeed have a past.

We couldn't possibly fit all the history of Corolla into this small book. If you want to learn more, the Currituck County Library, in the county office building on Highway 12, or local bookstores can steer you toward books of local interest.

Norris Austin

NORRIS AUSTIN'S
COROLLA STORIES

Norris Austin is a seventh-generation Outer Banker, a descendant of Thomas Austin, who was shipwrecked on Hatteras Island in the late 1700s, thus firmly establishing the Austin clan on the Outer Banks. The Austin name moved to Corolla in 1891 when William Riley Austin, Norris's grandfather, moved from Hatteras to Corolla to become lightkeeper at the Currituck Beach Lighthouse. Since then, the Austins have had a permanent footing in Corolla. William Riley Austin's son, John Austin, who is Norris's father, spent his life in Corolla, except for the few years he served in World War I.

Norris, too, spent his life in Corolla. He has lived in Corolla village longer than anybody else. He is not the oldest resident of the area, but he has lived there continuously longer than any of the other few longtime residents.

Norris was born on April 5, 1938. His parents, John and Virginia Austin, made their home in the quiet village of Corolla. Virginia delivered Norris at Norfolk General Hospital, the closest hospital to Corolla. Norris was a premature baby and had to spend the first month of his life

in the Norfolk hospital, but that was one of only two short spells of his life that he was not living in Corolla.

Norris still lives in the heart of Corolla village, a seashell's throw from his childhood home and schoolhouse, surrounded in part by lifelong memories of the past and in part by the drastic change of the present time.

In 68 years, Norris has seen Corolla change many times over, but none of the changes have been more drastic than the development of this area since the 1990s. But Norris is not bitter about the change. He accepts the change and generously shares his memories of old Corolla with anyone who is interested. He volunteers at The Whalehead Club in the summer, giving tours and informing people about the history of the historic clubhouse and this area.

In the winter of 2006, Norris agreed to record some of his memories and stories about growing up in Corolla. I sat down with Norris numerous times and talked about the past and the way things were. Each time we met, Norris remembered more and more details about life on the Currituck Outer Banks in the old days. What follows here are Norris's stories about his life as well as some photographs from his family collections. We re-organized the stories into general categories because they seemed to flow better that way, but everything that follows is from Norris. You may want to read the overview of the history of Corolla in this book before reading the stories, as that may help you understand the context better. We hope that you enjoy Norris's stories as much as we do.

--- Molly Harrison

Family History

My family came to Corolla in 1891. My grandparents were from Hatteras. My grandfather was in the lighthouse service at Cape Hatteras and was transferred to Corolla as assistant keeper at the Currituck Beach Lighthouse. My dad was three months old at that time. My dad's name was John Wendell Austin. My grandparents had three boys when they moved to Corolla, and later they had four girls. They lived in the duplex building that was part of the lighthouse service. I've always heard that they lived on the north side. My father told me several times that he was raised in the little attic on the third floor -- that was his bedroom.

My grandparents kept their kids at home. You know, so they weren't out doing things they weren't supposed do. They always had something to keep them busy. Every day they had certain chores to do before they could go out and play. I've heard daddy say that they had to take a pocket knife and go around about once a week and cut the grass that was growing between the bricks on the walkways.

Long ago in the village, the government had a school for the lighthouse and Coast Guard kids, and the fishermen families had their own separate school. Then the two schools merged. I think they had already merged when my dad started school.

My dad had two brothers and four sisters, so it was a big family. Daddy, Uncle Pell and Uncle Edgar were the main ones who lived here in Corolla all the time. Uncle Pell was in the Coast Guard and he was always traveling around, but he kept his home here until about the mid-1940s.

Norris Austin, second from the right with his mother, friends and kittens.

Photo Courtesy: Norris Austin

Norris's grandparents, Wiliam Riley Austin and Lovie Peele Austin. William Riley Austin was the keeper of the Currituck Beach Lighthouse from 1891 to 1929.

Then he moved to the mainland, because of the school more than anything. Uncle Edgar died in 1931 of appendicitis. Aunt Fannie married one of the Johnson boys and he was at the Coast Guard station here, so she lived here for a while. My aunts Jennie, Ruth and Gertie got married and moved away from Corolla. You know, I heard all their stories growing up, but when you're small you don't really pay attention. They'd all get together and reminisce about growing up. It sounds like it was a real happy village then, full of nice people.

I was told of a funny episode about when my grandfather was the lightkeeper at the lighthouse. There were groups from the mainland that came on excursions, most of them were Sunday school classes or groups from the churches. They would come over on Sunday and walk up the lighthouse stairs. On one occasion, this young couple was having a lover's spat. There they were up on the outer deck of the lighthouse, and she was not really having much to do with him. "Well," the boy said, "If you don't love me, I'll just climb over and kill myself." And he started to act like he was going to climb over the railing. My grandfather came over and grabbed him by the seat of the pants and jokingly said, "Here, son, let me help you get over." And the guy just crumbled down on his knees.

My grandfather was in the lighthouse service from 1891 to 1929. Then he moved

Lovie Austin with John Austin (Norris's father) and Jennie Austin (Norris's aunt).

over to the village and bought a house and some property. When he was at the lighthouse, he had built a kitchen off in the yard. That's because back then people didn't like to cook food in the house and they liked the kitchen to be set off in case of fires. He moved that kitchen building from the lighthouse compound and joined it onto his house in the village, making a kitchen, dining room, den and porch. The house is still here in the village and my nephew lives there now.

I was born in April and my grandfather died in September. I heard my mother say that she'd come in and set me on his bed and he'd feel of my arms and say I was going to make a football player or prize fighter. He knew I was going to be a big guy. I was about 8 years old when

my grandmother died. I knew her very well. Her name was Lovie Austin. I don't remember her ever talking about her days at the lighthouse much. She was a real kind person. She helped a lot of people who were sick. After my grandpa died she more or less went around visiting between her seven children. She stayed with Aunt Jennie and Aunt Fannie for long periods of time and she passed away at one of their homes. Now there are people who say that my grandmother Lovie haunts the keepers' house! I don't think that's true at all, and my family is offended by that tale. I would think she has better things to do in the after life.

My father had good memories of growing up at the lighthouse. He was three months old when he moved there and he was 30 something when his parents moved away from the lighthouse. So except for his years in the Army, he spent most all of his life near the lighthouse. It always was a home to him, and a place that he really agonized over seeing getting run down when the state didn't keep it up. Daddy was real happy to see Outer Banks Conservationists restoring the keepers' house in the 1970s, but he passed away in 1981 before he could see the restoration completed.

My father went in the Army in World War I and when he got out he came back to Corolla. At first, he ran a business of buying and selling fish and ducks. The ducks were shipped up north for the restaurants. Mainly he got his supply of fish and ducks buying them from other people. He would put them in these wooden barrels, just open their stomachs and take their intestines out and put a layer of salt in and ship them off on the Comet. The old Comet was a steamboat that used to come down the sound, and it would bring freight to the village and pick up freight to take to the mainland.

JW Austin Store

In 1935 my dad was named postmaster in Corolla. He was the postmaster and my mom was assistant postmaster. At that time, post offices were small and were in stores, and the postmasters had to furnish their own equipment and boxes. Dad bought Mr. Sol Sanderlin's store and gas station and all his post office equipment when Mr. Sanderlin was retiring as postmaster.

Dad called his store JW Austin Store. It was on Knapp House Road.

Mr. Sanderlin also had what he called a landing house at the State Dock, and Dad bought the landing house too. That was where the barge would unload the gas barrels for the gas station. There was such a good channel coming in at that time that the barge from Poplar Branch could come right up to the State Dock. The barge would come in loaded down with gas and kerosene, and Dad would roll the barrels of gas and kerosene

Photo Courtesy: Norris Austin

into the landing house. Then he'd load four or five barrels into his truck and take them back to the store. He would have to handpump the gas into the big tank at the store. Then he had one of those old glass containers that would pump out five gallons of gas at a time. He sold gas from the Esso/Standard Oil Company. Most everybody in the village had a car.

When I was growing up my dad had a thirty-foot shad boat with a small cabin on it. He anchored it off in the boat basin at the State Dock, and he had a skiff he would shove out to it. He used it to go across the sound to Poplar Branch and get things to sell in the store. He'd load the boat full of supplies. I went with him on those trips before I was in school. I remember several thunderstorms we got into going to Poplar Branch. In the summertime thunderstorms would come up out of nowhere. Currituck Sound can get very violent.

JW Austin in his store.

The store sold a lot of things -- candy, BCs, aspirin, sardines, Vienna sausages, crackers, toiletries. During the war the store was the PX for the Coast Guard, and he had to sell what they wanted. After the war

Enjoy a delicious
stewart
**HOT
SANDWICH**

HAM & CHEESE	85¢	HOT DOG	60¢
TORPEDO	95¢		
PIZZA	65¢		
CHEESEBURGER	65¢		

Norris Austin at the JW Austin store in the 1960s.

l feed and chicken feed. I remember back in those days the chicken feed used to be in these print check bags, and a lot of women would take them and make dresses. Later, my dad was turning more to driving his truck to Elizabeth City and Norfolk rather than going across the sound. I think it was actually quicker to go up the beach and then drive over to Elizabeth City rather than drive down through Duck. I remember seeing him come down the beach with the back of his truck full of soft drinks. He got his candy at the W.H. Weatherly Candy Company in Elizabeth City.

My father was always very well-liked. He had a way of making everybody feel good. He had a knack of what to say or do to make people feel good. He was a very neat and proper person. He almost always had his necktie on. He said he never felt dressed unless he had his necktie on.

I think I knew most everybody in town. Before I went to school, I was either at the store or in the yard next to the store. Our house was right beside the store, and we had a big fenced yard with a little dune where I played. I remember a babysitter who just sat around and read novels while I played. I remember in the store my parents had this old ice box for drinks, the kind you put a cake of ice in to keep the drinks cool. Right next to that they had this box that was just big enough for me to crawl around and play in while they worked. I remember several times a sailor coming in and saying, "Well, how much is the kid in the box?" It kind of gave me a little scare at first until I realized they were kidding.

Dad ran that little store up until the 1970s, though I became the postmaster in 1959. You know, people always tell me that they thought the Austins were the only postmasters in Corolla, but that's not true. The first postmaster was Mrs. Emma Parker. Then Mr. S.C. Gray. Then Mr. Harold Hampton. Then Sol Sanderlin, then my dad, then me until 1992. Then it was Linda Lewis.

My father retired as postmaster on July 31, 1959, and I was appointed postmaster on August 1. I took the store over around 1979 and ran both the store and the post office.

The Village Life

The main road that went through Corolla village was Corolla Village Road, which is still here. Right where you went into The Whalehead Club, there was a road that went down to the State Dock, or community dock, and the lighthouse dock. The State Dock had places to tie up boats, and people always kept their boats there. Ten to 15 boats were there all the time when I was little. My dad's landing house was between the two docks.

Right north of where the chapel is now, Corolla Village Road went into a Y and became Jones's Hill Road, and that was mainly the beach access road. There was a big sand dune – Jones's Hill – at the end of the road that was encroaching over into the road. By the 1960s, it was getting very hard to get through there because of the sand moving into the road, so the state made a beach access road over by the lighthouse. They took 30 feet from the lighthouse property and 30 feet from The Whalehead Club property and extended Corolla Village Road out to the beach. That is still the only public vehicular access to the beach. Schoolhouse Road

Photo Courtesy: Norris Austin

Sand from Jones Hill (now gone) creeping into the village.

was not there when I was growing up. There was an oak tree that was in the middle of where Schoolhouse Road is now. Just about every kid in the village had carved their initials into it. It was knocked down probably about 1973 or so when they built Schoolhouse Road. Knapp House Road was the other road in the village, but it's gone now. It connected to Corolla Village Road about where the Scarborough house's cedar tree is now. My father's store was on Knapp House Road. Mrs. Henley's store was just across the street.

The mail came by boat when I was little. Visitors would often come in on the mailboat. If someone came to the village I was always curious. I always wanted to meet them. We had people that would come in and just camp out on the beach in a tent. And there were always people walking down the beach from Virginia. If they looked hungry, somebody would feed them; the villagers were always good to them. There was one guy, Lockheed, and his partner, Burgess. They were with the Mariner's Museum in Newport News.

They used to come over on the mailboat. They wrote hundreds of things about this place. They were always here. At least you could look for them in the spring.

There were probably 30 or so houses then, on Corolla Village Road and Jones's Hill Road, and out by the [Currituck Beach] Coast Guard station. A lot of people had moved in during the Depression because they could always get a fish or something to eat here. But then times started getting better, and people started migrating out of Corolla to the cities. Every year another family would move away.

World War II

Some of my first memories are of the time during World War II, when I was about three or four years old. Corolla was very different during the war because there were a lot of people here. The Coast Guard had set up a training center at The Whalehead Club. New trainees would come in every six to eight weeks then be sent out into service. There were 300 or so men at the clubhouse. A lot of the trainers who were stationed here brought their families with them. They would rent anything for their families to stay in. They would rent barns, an extra bedroom, anything. The first year I started school in 1945, there were 60 children in the school, most of them from Coast Guard families.

Dad's store was the PX for the servicemen. Two times a day, the men had breaks and were allowed to come to the store. But it was a little store and everyone couldn't fit in there at once, so they had to line up and come in six or so at a time. There would be an MP supervising. I have seen men two in line all the way from the store to the clubhouse, waiting for their supplies. During WWII sugar was rationed, but because Daddy's store was the PX for the Coast Guard, he could sell all the candy the servicemen wanted.

When the mail came in, my parents would have to lock the door and sort out all the mail. Almost 75 percent of it went back to the Coast Guard training center at The Whalehead Club. They'd put it in bags and an officer would come and pick it up. Most post offices depended on the revenue for what the postmaster's salary was. Then later the salary depended on the number of cancellations. But all this mail that my parents had to handle was free mail because they didn't charge the servicemen. He couldn't get the credit for all that mail.

During World War II, one thing I remember is that we had blackouts at night. You couldn't have a light on inside unless you had blackout shades. You couldn't show any light from your window because that would silhouette the village from the ocean for the enemy ships offshore. The lighthouse was not in operation then either. Most everyone had the old kerosene lights in those days. My dad had a generator that he'd run to provide electricity for the washing machine and the refrigeration. But most people just used kerosene lamps to sit around and talk. There was no television. Corolla didn't get electricity until 1955.

I remember one time that an oil tanker was bombed out in the ocean just off of Corolla, and the burning fire lit up all of Corolla. I wasn't scared because my parents never showed that they were afraid. Right now if I knew the enemy was less than a half-mile from me I think it would be real frightening. I know they must have been afraid too, but they never showed any fear around us.

You could travel the beach at night, but you had to travel by starlight. You weren't allowed to have your car headlights on. About every two or three miles you would be stopped by the shore patrol. They were on horseback and they'd come out from behind the dunes. You didn't joke with them. It was very serious. They were just young men and they were scared, they knew how serious it was to be on the lookout for spies or the enemy. You had to show the shore patrol your citizen's card and know the password. Starting down from Virginia Beach, they'd give you a password and then about every three miles down you'd be stopped and they'd give you another password.

Family Life

Life in Corolla was similar to a farm life because we had gardens and livestock. Most everybody in the village raised their own meats, like chicken and turkeys and hogs. And everybody had a garden. It was just part of the household.

My mother had a great garden. I had to help water it and weed the grass out of it, and help with the picking. My mother worked hard at the canning. She canned what we needed all year -- snap beans, tomatoes, corn and all the vegetables.

We also had chickens so we always had fresh eggs. Some were fryer chickens that we'd fry on Sunday. And some were older, which would lay eggs. And then when they got too old to lay, we had stew chickens. We always had one or two hogs that we would put up for winter meat and salt pork. Slaughtering the animals was always kind of heart breaking for me. You get used to feeding it and then one morning you walk out and shoot it. I didn't like that.

When I was older I raised hogs for several people who wanted them for meat. We had all the hog-cleaning equipment. It's a lot of work for a hog cleaning. You have to scrape the hair off them. All the meat has to be cut up, and you have to hang them. Most of the time the women would be cutting and grinding the meat for sausage. The tenderloin was always what everybody wanted first. I always liked the stew. You take the liver and some other meat and put dumplings and potatoes in it. It was really good.

A group of school kids in Corolla in the 1940s

Photo Courtesy: Norris Austin

We ate well when I was growing up. My mother was always excellent at frying chicken. When I was growing up I didn't think there was anything like fresh fried chicken right out of the yard. We often had roast beef for Sunday dinner. My mother made hot biscuits three times a day. We didn't have sliced loaf bread back then. We ate a lot of fried fish. There was some fish like rockfish and drum that we'd make Outer Banks style -- boil it in water, add potatoes, then fry meat grease and add cracklins to it. That was really good eating.

You couldn't get oysters up this far, so people would give them to us. People would give you a lot of things in those days. If someone from Wanchese came up they'd bring oysters because they knew we didn't have them. Crabs were plentiful. And we got clams when it got cold. It was always pretty healthy eating. We had plenty of good food.

There were a lot of fruit trees and figs too. When you have fig trees, and the figs are ripe, you always want people to pick all the figs so you don't have to eat and preserve so many. The way it worked was that people would ask you if they could engage the picking of your figs. So you'd give them a specific day to come pick all the figs on the tree. I remember once this lady told me she'd like to have some figs. So I said, well, come over on Wednesday or Thursday. She comes and she has no container or anything. I said, "Well what are you going to put all these figs in?" She said, "Oh, I only wanted four!" That's the difference between a city girl and a country boy. She wasn't used to engaging figs. If she just wanted four she could have come by anytime.

Feral hogs would come into the village every now and then and root in the gardens. Everybody up here had a fence around their yard to keep the animals out.

If you wanted to keep a garden you had to have a fence.

There were a lot of people up here whose livestock just roamed free. Most everybody had a registered mark on their animals. Each person had a trademark notch on their animals' ears. One person's trademark might be three notches, another person's might be a single slit. There were free-roaming cows; it seemed like the cows always liked to walk head into the wind. I remember just a few free-roaming horses. We didn't know that they were Spanish mustangs or anything like that. I didn't know if they were wild or belonged to somebody or what. We didn't think about them very much. Most people's animals ran free until they passed the "no fence" laws. That really doesn't make sense because it's just the opposite. The laws meant that you had to put your animals in a fence instead of letting them roam.

Things Unique to Corolla Village Life

People did various things for a living in Corolla. Some people were in the Coast Guard. Some would work as marsh guards for The Whalehead Club or other hunt clubs. The marsh guards would spend days down in these houses in the marsh, looking for trespassers. Sometimes some of the hunt clubs would feed the waterfowl, and the marsh guards would do that too. Then you had fishing guides. When I was growing up bass fishing was real popular in Currituck Sound. This area was called the "sportsman's paradise."

People would come a long ways to go bass fishing here. So we had bass fishing guides and hunting guides.

There was a lot more waterfowl when I was growing up. We didn't have all these developments along the shoreline, and there wasn't as much environmental pollution then. The rules and regulations have changed so much since then. There's always been a limit on shooting, but it varied from year to year. When I was a boy my dad had a great goose blind. I don't ever remember going to that blind when we didn't get at least something. But now you can go out there and stay all day and you might not get anything. It's gotten so that now you are very lucky to get your limit. The ducks and geese have become more or less educated about what duck blinds are. There's been a lot of changes. Back in the old days you could have as many blinds as you wanted. Then they made a law that you could only have two blinds per person. A lot of guides had to get a license for their wives, so their wives would take out a couple of blinds and they'd have four blinds per family.

The visiting sportsmen and hunters would stay at The Whalehead Club and at Mr. Cleveland Lewark's Lighthouse View Hunt Club. A little bit farther up the Guggenheim family had a club. Some people in the village would take in borders and furnish them guides.

Driving

We always drove on the beach, either to get to Norfolk or to go visiting down the Outer Banks. People just knew how to drive on the beach, they knew how to accelerate at the proper rate. Nobody ever got stuck. Dad had a 1940 Dodge truck

Norris coming back after a day of hunting.

that we'd drive up the beach to Norfolk. I don't remember us ever getting stuck. If there was a bad nor'easter or the tide was too high to use the beach, you could take the Pole Road, which was the interior road that the Coast Guard used to tend their telephone poles and wires. The Pole Road ran all the way down the coast to Hatteras but it was full of holes. I was probably about 12 when I first started driving, on the beach. These were state roads back here in the village, so you weren't really allowed to be on them if you weren't properly licensed. If we met a car while I was driving on the beach, my dad would make me stop and he would take over.

Phones

The village didn't get household telephone service until 1969. We always had a phone, though, because daddy was the postmaster. So he had the phone in our house. It was the old crank up kind, and we had five people on our line. Of course you heard all their rings. Ours was three longs. You rung in at the Virginia Beach Coast Guard Station, and they would plug you in to where you wanted to go. Neighbors came to use our phone, but it had to be an emergency. You didn't call just to chit-chat. It was a party line, so if someone picked up while you were talking you would lose hearing power. My dad would never have let us eavesdrop on anyone else's conversations.

Schoolhouse

Before I started school, I would always be out playing in our yard, which was very close to the schoolhouse. At lunch time, when the kids came out on the playground to play for an hour, I would sneak off out of our yard and go over there. Mrs. Coward, the teacher, she'd usually come and block me when I'd come over. She'd give me an apple and say "Norris, go back home."

Kids at school in the 1940s. Norris is the second from the left.

She'd say "I'll watch you, though." So I got tired of that because I wanted to stay and play. So I decided I was going to write her a note from my mother. I took out a sheet of paper and a crayon and went around and around in circles, and I thought I was writing her a note. I went over and I said, "Mrs. Coward, I have a note from my mother." She said, "Oh you do?" And I said "Yes." She opened it and read, "Dear Mrs. Coward, Please give Norris an apple and send him straight home." I said, "Is that what it says!?" She said, "That's what it says." I said, "It's supposed to say, 'Give Norris an apple and let him stay and play.'" She said, "Well it says to give you an apple and send you straight home." I was so puzzled that I could've written that. She said she'd watch me until I got back home.

I started first grade at Corolla School in 1945. There were about 60 children in all the grades, mainly the children of Coast Guard families. The local students came from Corolla village and from Wash Woods and Penny's Hill, which was called Seagull. There was a school bus that went up the beach to pick them up. My first teacher, Mrs. Coward, had taught here for seven years straight, and the first year I went to school was the only year I had her. She left after that. Ms. Grace Lewark was my second grade teacher and I had her again in the 11th grade, but all the years I was in school I had a new teacher every year. In fact, a couple years we had two teachers because the teacher left in the middle of the term.

The Corolla School was a one-room schoolhouse, and one teacher taught all grades. It was kind of interesting because you could hear someone in another grade reciting their subjects while you were waiting to be called up to do your lessons. The teachers usually tried to keep the smaller children busy. We had to take an hour, hour and a half's nap in the afternoon in the cloak room in the back.

They had cots in there. I hated that. I liked to talk so it was always hard for me to shut up and get some sleep. But we were required to take a nap. And we had a long table that we could do artwork and stuff like that. I know I was always interested in what the other students were doing. Listening to different recitals was probably the biggest thing with me.

Right after the war, the number of students probably went down to about 30 because the Coast Guard families left. A lot of the kids in the school came from The Whalehead Club. Mr. Adams, who owned The Whalehead Club, took in several German families after the war. He sponsored them in this country, and they worked for him. They lived in houses he had moved out to his compound. They all had kids. At one time there could have been almost as many German kids as American kids at our school. I really don't know how we did it, but we got along fine. They only had a crash course in English. They couldn't understand our Outer Banks drawl, and we couldn't understand them, but I don't remember us having a communication barrier. I still see about three or four of them, every once in a while some of them will come by. In a one-room school like that you kind of grow up like a family. You feel like you're kin to everyone.

One of the main things we missed at a one-room school was the fact that we didn't have a lot of sports, no football or basketball or games like that. I remember one game we called Auntie Over. And we had volleyball nets. We played baseball. The first two years I was there we had lunch in the south room. Mrs. Twiford from the village made us homemade biscuits, ham and cabbage and stuff like that. Nice meals for a nickel, I think. Then after that some kids went home for lunch. I always wanted to eat at school because I thought it was fun to bring your lunch. But most of the time I went home.

To raise money for our school, we'd always have a play, usually in the wintertime in the hunt season because we could invite the hunters who were visiting the area. They always helped us out. We didn't charge admission, but they would make a donation. I remember a play about Johnny Appleseed. I played his father once. Put flour in my hair. Mr. Lewark had an old-timey living room suit from the 1800s and he always lent it to us for the play. They really were good plays. We used the money we took in to buy library books and playground equipment. We had a good library. We really needed a library more than ever in a place like this. Just when you'd read everything twice, the plays would generate enough money to get a new supply of books.

The teachers had to take an upper hand to keep all the kids under control. That might be why we had so many teachers. I'm sure it was really hard. But back then, the parents supported the teachers. No matter what the teacher said you didn't have a chance. I grew up about a three-minute walk from the schoolhouse. I was so close that they could always send to get my dad out of the post office if I misbehaved.

In the schoolhouse we had this big coal stove in the middle of the floor. Sometimes, just to aggravate the teacher and disrupt class, some of the older kids would take the eraser off of their pencil and drop it on the coal stove. There'd be this awful burnt rubber smell. So everybody would have to go outside until

Miss Anna Mae Mooreland from Tennesee came to Corolla to teach in the school in the 1940s. She had never seen the ocean and did not have the upper hand witht the kids.

the offensive smell cleared out.

I remember my ninth grade teacher, Miss Anna Mae Mooreland from Tennessee. She didn't totally have the upper hand. Sometimes at lunchtime when we were outside, all of us kids would just leave and run out to the beach. She'd go down there chasing behind us. One day we all took off and were well ahead of her, and she was catching up with this one boy, Donald. The rest of us made it back to the schoolhouse before the teacher and Donald got back. About that time the mailboat came in carrying Mrs. Brumsey, one the administrators from the superintendent's office. She came over from the mainland for visits from time to time. Just as we had gotten back to the school, we saw her coming down the road with the mailman in the mail truck! So we scrambled to our desks, opened our books and got real quiet. When she

opened the door and came in we were all just very studious. Nobody looked behind, we just sat there reading our books. Finally she said, "Good evening, children." We said, "Oh! Hello, Mrs. Brumsey. How are you?" Like we had been so busy studying that this was the first time we'd seen her. She said, "Where is your teacher?" And we said, "We don't know. She was going down to the beach or something." She said, "Does she do that often." "Oh yes ma'am," we said. And about that time the door opened and Donald came running in and Anna Mae came in and tripped and fell on the floor. She was carrying a board that she was going to hit Donald with. And then she saw Mrs. Brumsey and started crying.

Then there was another teacher I remember who we played an April Fool's trick on. There used to be a lot of wasps that were up in the attic of the schoolhouse that would come down when it got real hot. If one wasp came down, everybody would want to disrupt the whole class, "Oh there's a wasp!!" and flail around and act like we were scared to death of it. And this teacher would say, "Oh, wasps don't hurt you. They won't sting you." On April Fool's Day, we all caught a bunch of wasps and wrapped them up in a box. We said to the teacher, "We have a present for you." She opened it up and the whole bunch of wasps came out. One or two stung her. She never had a fit about us getting excited over wasps again. She got the message.

On the last day of school every year, we always had picnics on the Knapp House porch. That was the only house out on the oceanfront. Mr. Knapp built the house in the late 1920s as a vacation home. It had a big porch all the way around.

As I got older, the number of kids at school kept dropping down until the last year that I was there I was the only senior in the school, and there were only 17 children in all the grades.

After Christmas of my senior year I had passed the state exam and covered all my subjects. But in order to have a graduation I went across the sound and stayed with my aunt and uncle and went my last half of the year at Griggs High School. Otherwise it would have been just me to graduate. Over there I made 21 students. The Corolla School closed about two years after I graduated. The rest of the kids, some of them went to Virginia Beach and some just quit school entirely. I graduated in 1955 so I'd have to say the school closed about 1957 or '58.

Entertainment

We did a lot of different things for entertainment when I was a kid. Of course swimming was a big thing – in the ocean. The beach was pretty well desolate. So we'd go over there and take our clothes off and go swimming. My parents and all the parents believed that right after you eat you were not supposed to go swimming. Well, that was the first thing we wanted to do. One time I remember I had to come home for something and my hair was wet. My mother caught on that I had been swimming and then I was restricted to stay home after eating.

We did a lot of beachcoming. It was a real rewarding time because there were always something new to explore out on the beach. Before the environmental laws about dumping trash in the ocean were enacted, the beach was a real mystery every day. One of the things that I was real interested in was these milk cartons that they used to have. They were really heavy waxed and they had a movie star's picture on it – Jane Russell, Roy Rogers, Dale Evans. I had a big collection of them that I found on the beach.

I started smoking by going out there because the Navy would throw these K-Ration tins overboard when they were going in to port in Hampton Roads, and the tins would wash up here on the beach. You could find K-Ration tins anytime. There would always be either Chesterfield, Lucky or Camels in the tins. I got to liking Lucky's so good that I made Lucky's my brand. If I didn't find Lucky's in one can, I would open cans till I found them. I was probably about 8 or 9 years old; it was after the war. The tins also had these milk tablets, and a little pudding cup -- some kind of dates or something, it was terrible -- and crackers. It was supposed to be that you could live off it for a couple of days if you had to.

We'd also find wood on the beach. If somebody wanted some boards for an outbuilding or animal pen, they just went over to the beach and got them. One time my uncle said that I was the richest guy he knew because I had mahogany hog pens. But I found the mahogany on the beach.

Photo Courtesy: Norris Austin

Hunting wild pigs in the 1950s.

A lot of times we'd find oranges and bananas. I felt real exotic coming home with a stalk of bananas on my back.

I used to like to go softshell crabbing. We waded off the shore to catch them. I used to catch them with my hands, but most people would use a crab net. I'd kind of go down in the grass and when I felt a soft crab I'd catch him. There were lots of crabs. They were always very good eating. We just kept them for our own use. The bank where they are developing Corolla Bay now was a really pretty bank for soft shell crabbing.

My dad had that 30-foot shad boat, and he would take us and his friends out fishing. On Sunday afternoon we'd go out to where the duck blinds were. That seemed to be a good place to catch white perch. And my dad was a great hunter. I used to hunt some too.

We had to have respect for other people's property, but other than that we could roam around. We'd go down to the State Dock and sit around. The schoolhouse grounds had a merry-go-round and slide and the things to exercise with. We were free to use those anytime. Of course the beach, we were free to enjoy anytime.

In the evenings people would visit at other people's homes and talk. You learned a lot about history from listening to people talk. I remember Franklin Roosevelt's Fireside Chats. At everybody's house they listened to the radio. You weren't allowed to whisper or anything during the Fireside Chats. My daddy also listened to news of the war with Gabriel Heater on the radio. Every night there was the war news. In my house we had to be real quiet.

I used to follow my dad around a lot. He'd haul his boat out at The Whalehead Club to scrape the barnacles off. He'd have to do it in early morning or late evening when he was not working. He'd tell me to stay home, but as soon as he left I'd go waddling down the road after him. They had a big gate by The Whalehead Club, and inside there they had a Chesapeake Retriever named Curly. Curly had bitten me a few times. I'd always crawl up on the gate and look to see where Curly was. If he was by the clubhouse, I could make it to my dad. My mother caught me on that fence a couple times and brought me home.

Occasionally on Sunday we'd go down to my grandparents in Nags Head Woods. Sometimes daddy would take me and my brother and we'd go to Hatteras and visit his folks down there. Mother and daddy couldn't travel at the same time because she was the assistant postmaster. When he was gone she had to work. But I would take trips with her too. We went to Washington and places like that in the summertime.

Whalehead Club

The Knights died in 1936, and Mr. Ray Adams bought the Corolla Island clubhouse and the surrounding property in 1940. Mr. Adams bought 3,000 acres from Mr. Knight's heirs, from the lighthouse down to where the traffic light at Timbuk II is now. He leased the clubhouse and some property to the Coast Guard during the war. I first remember the house when the Coast Guard was there. They showed some of the first outdoor movies I'd ever seen. They projected them up on a screen on the side of the house. There were also movies out at the Coast Guard station on Saturday mornings for 25 cents.

The house was always pretty active. Mr. Adams was in the meat-packing business in Washington. He had guests there all year round. He had a good relationship with congressmen and senators. Jack Dempsey came a lot because he used to hunt. Mr. Adams flew in often, but Mrs. Adams came mostly in

the summer. A lot of people came in the summer as well as the winter. Mr. Adams had all these people who lived and worked there and grew his vegetables. He had a dairy farm there, with some cows fenced in. My mother had a cow and after she got rid of it, they would give her a gallon of milk a lot of times.

In 1950 Mr. Adams put in an airstrip on the southside of the clubhouse. When they were working out there they found a whale's head. So that's why he changed the name from Corolla Island to The Whalehead Club. How the whale's head got there I don't know. He would fly people in on his landing strip. Before that, they had landed on the beach, so we were used to seeing planes.

The Whalehead Club was a big part of my growing up. Mr. Adams's oldest granddaughter and I were very close friends when I was older, and I was there quite often to see her. She stayed there a lot in the summer. Old Curly was still there then and I had to watch out for him. I had grown up seeing that house. I don't know if I had any specific thoughts about it. It was a nice house. It was just there.

Mr. Adams planted the pine trees you see in Corolla village today. He gave us kids a dollar in the afternoon and we'd plant trees for him. He planted thousands of pine trees. Nobody thought they'd live but they did. From my home in the village, from our upstairs room, we used to could look out and see the ocean and the Coast Guard Station. It was bald out there. But now you can't see the ocean at all from the village because the pine trees are so thick. The reason was that he wanted them was to raise a lot of pheasants here. He had a man from Pennsylvania come down to poison all the foxes and predators because

*In the 1950s Mr. Adams built an airstrip and would fly
people in to the Whalehead Club.*

he put out all these pheasants. Our dog got poisoned. He really wanted those pheasants. The pheasants took hold for a couple of years. You'd be walking down the road and one of the pheasants would jump up and make this awful noise and scare the daylights out of you.

In Mrs. Knight's swimming pool, Mr. Adams made a bullfrog pond. He brought in Mexican bullfrogs. They had these big old legs. I ate them one time. I went over with some of the boys from the Navy who were stationed at the lighthouse, and we speared the frogs and cooked them. They were actually good. The boy who was cooking them knew what he was doing.

Mr. Adams died in 1957. It was after he died that the property started going into real estate hands. Developers cut out

a portion and developed that. Whalehead Beach, Monteray Shores, Buck Island -- all of that was originally Mr. Knight's then Mr. Adams' property.

After Mr. Adams passed away, the Corolla Academy Boys' School leased The Whalehead Club for a while – from 1958 to 1963, in the summer months only. I worked at the academy in 1959. I'd go over about 5 in the morning and start breaking eggs for their breakfast. Then I would serve breakfast. I had to go to the post office at 9. And then in the evening I'd help serve at the steam table for their dinner. And I ran the dishwasher. The boys were pretty nice. Most of them were from very rich families and they'd always had a nanny and never saw their parents. This was the first time I ever realized that there were people who'd get someone else to raise their kids. The boys would come to my parents' store. A lot of them used to write to my mother because she'd be so good to them at the store. She'd always be real kind to them. They kind of adopted her as a mom.

Then the Atlantic Research company offered the owners more money than the school could afford, so Atlantic Research leased The Whalehead Club property. They later bought the property. Atlantic Research was doing a contract for the Air Force, part of the big race to get to the moon in the 1960s. Atlantic Research was making a solid propellant. Scientists and Air Force personnel stayed at the Whalehead Club, and Shirley Austin, my cousin's wife, cooked for them. Atlantic Research had a plant all the way down where the Food Lion is now, and the plant workers drove in from Virginia Beach.

There was a launching pad in the middle of the property where they would static fire these 9,000 pound rockets. They had to fire when wind was offshore so the smoke would go to sea. It sounded like Cape Canaveral. You could probably hear it in Elizabeth City. The rocket didn't blast off, it was static fire, bolted down. It was amazing to see. Atlantic Research left in the 1970s. After that a development group bought The Whalehead Club almost instantly and started developing the property.

The Lighthouse

In 1939 the lighthouse was automated and the keeper was removed. The Coast Guard came and charged the batteries, but no one was stationed there. I remember during the war they had a big horse stable behind the keepers' house where the gift shop is now. That was because the shore patrol rode horses. The keeper's house was full of hay.

When I was growing up the Coast Guard at Caffey's Inlet was in charge of the lighthouse. Every Monday, Wednesday and Friday they had to come and charge the batteries. Often at lunch break when I was older a bunch of us kids would go to the lighthouse, and the Coast Guard guy would let us go up. We went quite often. We just went up top and looked around to see if we could see the teacher and holler at her. We just looked around at the houses in the village and at the Knapp House on the beach.

Then there would be occasions where people would come as a group to the lighthouse. The Coast Guard would meet them there. College kids and people like that. They were more or less just visiting. For a while there was a Navy station right beside the tower. The Keepers' House just sat there and fell apart.

The Church

The Corolla Chapel was built in 1885 by the community members to be interdenominational. But somebody went over to the mainland and had it registered as a Baptist church. This caused a division in the community. In the 1930 the Baptists gave up the church because the circuit preacher had given it up. My father was listed as the trustee. My parents always kept the Corolla Chapel ready for a service. Daddy painted it and put on a new roof. My mother cleaned and dusted the inside. Visiting ministers would come through Corolla and preach for us from time to time, but we never had a full-time minister. We did have Sunday School and

Bible stories every Sunday. One of the visiting preachers when I was growing up was George Willis. He was a Coast Guard chaplain. He would go from station to station and hold services at the station for them. He always managed to come here and hold a service, and then he'd stay at our house.

In the 1960s the county was going to have to sell the church for tax money if someone didn't take it over, so the county attorney called my father and my father straightened up the tax bill in his name. He wanted it to always be a church. Then Daddy deeded the church over to me because he trusted me to make sure it remained a church. In 1987 I let Pastor John Strauss hold interdenominational services there. They were so popular that we outgrew the church. I told them that we could move the church, and our congregation moved it across the street and added on to it. The congregation, which I'm a part of, now owns it.

I remember when World War II ended, we all went to the church from school. They rang the bell and rang the bell and people from all over the village came. It was a real emotional time. People were crying and laughing and just glad it was over. The same thing happened when President Roosevelt died. People were very sad when he died.

Later Life

After I finished high school I started working for a while at Rice's department store in downtown Norfolk. Then I went to Kee's Coastal Business College and took Junior Accounting and General Business. I went to school because I wanted to do exactly what I did. I wanted

to be postmaster, and my dad encouraged me to go to school first. I didn't think I missed Corolla when I was gone, but I did. I always knew I wanted to come back to Corolla. The city was OK for a while, but it just wasn't like Corolla. Too many people. There was just something about Corolla that was special. I could hunt then, and I liked to fish a little. It was just a comfortable place. It was familiar. If someone started a car up the road, I knew exactly who it was by the sound of their engine, and I liked that.

I took over my father's job as postmaster in 1959. The population in the 1960s was really low as people migrated to the city. And it got to the point where duck hunting had gone down and people couldn't make a living here anymore as guides and had to move away. But we've always had little spurts in our economy, like the Boys' School and Atlantic Research, that gave everyone jobs. That kept the economy churning just a little bit. I worked two jobs for a long, long time. I needed to because the salaries just weren't that great. But I could live here if I worked two jobs.

I worked at the Corolla Boys' Academy for a while. And I worked at Atlantic Research as a security officer. I went there at 4 o'clock in the evening and worked until midnight. I had to go down to the plant and make sure the doors were locked, and there were machines I had to check. The research employees were not allowed to go into the plant area and work in their street clothes. And when they came back out they had to leave their work clothes and take a shower. They were working with brillium. Part of my job was to wear a mask and gloves and take their dirty work clothes and wash and

Norris Austin became postmaster of Corolla in 1959.

dry them and hang them on the racks for the next day.

I worked with animals a lot. Goats always fascinated me from when I was a boy on up. I liked the way they handled themselves -- they eat grass, they have a cud like a cow so they just stand and chew, they like to get up on high places. It's not true that they eat garbage, at least not any that I ever owned. They were always very dainty eaters. When I was about 25 years old I had a little over 100 goats. They started getting out of my pound I had down here in the village and going across the road and eating people's flowers. So the people that owned The Whalehead Club at that time told me that I could let them range free over their property. I went down to about where Monteray Shores is now, and there was an old guard house there. I put the goats out there. I'd go once a week and take them a five gallon bucket of corn. I'd call them all and

pet them and feed them and hang around with them a couple of hours so they were used to me. After they were down there about six or seven years people came and started stealing them. There were also some dogs from the Currituck Club that were getting into them. The dogs ran a few goats out onto the beach and the goats would drown rather than get caught by a dog. So I got them up and sold them.

Also I raised hogs. There were a lot feral or wild hogs in the area. I used to build traps much like a rabbit trap. You could always pretty well figure on catching a feral hog on a stormy night if you had some fish from the beach, like when somebody had pulled in a net of fatbacks. I trapped them up the road around acorn trees. They stayed in the marsh a lot in the summer months, but in the winter you'd find them up around the acorn trees. You could put out corn for them. But they really liked something that had an odor, like a rotten fish. I wouldn't want to eat them right out of the woods because they'd been living on fish and stuff like that. Later on, there were people coming from everywhere to go hog hunting here and they'd have barbecues and eat them right out of the woods. I wouldn't. They were much better if you put them in a pen and cleansed them out.

I got about 20 sow hogs at a time that I kept and tamed. They were really easy to domesticate. Once you brought them home and started feeding them every day and scratching them behind their ears, they'd fall out and want you to scratch their stomachs. A lot of people thought they were piney rooters, but they weren't. They were really feral hogs that people had left behind.

I would take a purebred boar to upgrade the bloodline, and I had a sort of pig factory for a long time. There was one or two always giving birth, and I'd raise

Norris and one of his pet goats.

them up to about 50 or 60 pounds and sell them. I was very attached to my animals though. I'd go out in the woods and rake pine straw for them when it was cold. The hogs would get in there and make a great big bed in the straw. It was funny to watch them. They'd all get bedded down and one would get too hot and they'd all have to shuffle around and rearrange themselves. One or two would get to talking ugly to the rest.

My little hog farm and farrowing house were right here in the village, and I enjoyed the work. But it was constant work of getting feed and feeding them, and I just quit after a while.

Currituck Banks Places and Names

Before my time, Corolla was called Jones's Hill, Whalehead Beach and Currituck Beach. When the village got a post office in 1885, the townspeople submitted those three names to the postal service. But the panel in Washington didn't like any of those names and asked the village to pick another name. Mr. Lewis Simmons, who was a schoolteacher here, suggested "Corolla." The term came from the inner part of a flower. There was an abundance of violet flowers at that time of the year, and Mr. Simmons said, "The inner circle of the flower is called a corolla. And we're sort of like that, an inner circle." So they sent that name in and that was what was accepted by the post office.

Jones Hill in the 1940s.

We were known as Cor-RAH-la up until Toyota made their car and now everybody wants to say "Cor-ROLL-a." But it's still Cor-RAH-la.

I never heard where the name Jones's Hill had come from. The Jones's Hill Life Saving Station was built in the 1880s, just north of where Corolla village is now. Of course, wherever there was a life saving station a little community formed around it. So that was why if you look at the very old pictures of Corolla, a lot of the village was up north of here, because the Jones's Hill station was north of here. In 1903 they built a new station south of here and called it the Currituck Beach Life Saving Station. They took the Jones's Hill station and moved it down there. The Currituck Beach station was on the ocean across from where The Whalehead Club is now.

Jones's Hill was just a great big sand dune. It was moving to the southwest and if the developers hadn't razed it down it would probably be over here in the village by now. North of Jones's Hill there was a lot of flat land that was not swampy but water stood on it. Developers filled all that

land in with the sand from Jones's Hill. That's the Villages at Ocean Hill now.

I remember playing on Jones's Hill. We'd just run up the hill and roll down. I hate to see them razing all the hills around here for development. A lot of people didn't realize that this was a whaling village in the 1800s, or maybe even earlier. People would go up on these high sand dunes and spot whales offshore. Then they would go to sea in their boats with harpoons and kill the whales and bring them in. They collected oil in the head and other parts of the whale to sell. Part of the whale was used to make perfume. Can you imagine, perfume from those smelly whales? That's why they called this area Whaleshead.

When I was growing up the Navy had what they called an anti-aircraft practice range about 3 miles north of Corolla. Whenever they were firing, they put a red flag up and you had to wait until they took the red flag up before you could go by on the beach. They fired these big brass anti-aircraft gunshells, about seven inches long. About five of them weighed about a pound. When I was growing up brass would sell for 60 cents a pound. After school a lot of us went over there and picked up the spent shells. We were making a good living selling them at Gutterman's in Norfolk. He wanted all the brass he could get. There was an old man that lived here who actually dug a tunnel in the side of a sand hill by the range. He would lie down in his tunnel and come out between rounds and try to grab shells. Many times the pilots would tell the Navy about the old man and they'd have to run him off. I think those Navy pilots got gun happy once in a while. They shot one or two of someone's cows a couple of times. The Navy had a practice range on the north end of Duck too.

Up north of Corolla, there was a settlement right there by Lewark's Hill. It was named for the Lewark family. Lewark's Hill, when I was growing up, was quite a place that people would come to for thrills. They'd drive up the hill and down the steep side. Every weekend it would be just solid with hot-rodders from Virginia Beach. In the '50s and '60s that was a big thing. We had a dog, Ivan, who stayed home with us Sunday night through Friday, but Friday afternoon he'd leave and go up to the hill. And he'd always hitch rides. He really did. People would say he'd just come right up and hop in their cars. He loved to ride that hill. I did it some for a while. I was riding with a friend and we had an accident with two vehicles. We spun and hit one. The car I was in rolled over about six times. We weren't either one hurt, but I decided that was enough.

Penny's Hill was another hill north of Corolla. The name Penny's Hill had something to do with the old Currituck Inlet. There's some legend about the old captains throwing pennies at the hill when they passed through the inlet, which closed long ago. Penny's Hill went down and covered up the old Seagull community in the woods. They had a right good-sized community. They had a Methodist Church and a cemetery. Then Penny's Hill spread all over it. I remember some parts of the community. A lot of people had to move their houses, or just give it up to the sand. The sand would just pack up to the back of their house and they just had to get out. We had children in our school from Seagull. It was probably in the late '40s and early '50s when the sand started coming in bad. I understand there were some big houses there. Old farm-type houses like there are in Corolla village.

Oceanfront

There wasn't much out on the oceanfront. The Knapps had a vacation house. And over by the Coast Guard station there were some houses. There wasn't a cottage line like there is now. Most all the older people on the Outer Banks built on the soundside. They didn't want the oceanfront. In fact, that was the cheapest part of their property. If you had come here in 1920 and wanted to buy oceanfront property you would have been very popular. They would have almost given it to you because it had no value. I remember when oceanfront development was starting. Carova Beach started first. Then Whalehead. Then Ocean Sands. We didn't know if they would last. We just kind of wondered.

South of Corolla

Right south of the Currituck Beach Coast Guard station was a big hill. A little bit before that was a bit of quicksand, and it was supposed to be fun to get stuck in the quicksand. I didn't think it was fun. I remember a horse got in the quicksand once and they had to shoot him.

Six miles south of the Currituck Beach station was the Poyner's Hill Coast Guard Station and a little community called Poyner's Hill. The Navy had a radio station there when I was small. When they closed up the Navy station, Mr. Adams moved the buildings up here to the oceanfront. That was what they used as the barracks for the Corolla Boys' Academy. The school-age children from the Poyner's Hill community went to school on the mainland at Poplar Branch. It was only a short way across the sound from there to Poplar Branch, and their daddy would take them across the sound to go to school. But sometimes the sound was frozen over and they had to come to Corolla School. The sound sometimes would freeze solid over. Some people would drive on it, but it was kind of risky.

Monkey Island

The Pamunkey Indians used to inhabit this area, and Monkey Island was named after them. If you go over there now you can see oyster beds that the Indians left behind. There are just a very few Pamunkey Indians left in the Yorktown area today. I know when I was growing up there was a couple of places that were called "Burying Grounds" over by the beach. We were always told not to bother them. We were supposed to show respect to those mounds. They've been built over now.

Monkey Island was always a part of Corolla. We more or less thought of it as being a part of us here. The Penn family from Reidsville, owners of the American Tobacco Co., owned the Monkey Island Club for years and years. Now Fish & Wildlife owns it, but they're not keeping it up. They're just letting it go. It's always been a fascinating place. It has lots of fruit trees – fig trees, apple and pear trees. Now they claim it's really infested with cottonmouth moccasins. The club is being very badly abused. People are writing grafitti on the walls, busting the windows. All that is heartbreaking to see.

Storms

Ash Wednesday storm was March 7, 1962. The day before, it was hazy, foggy. I went to Virginia Beach that morning and came back in the afternoon. There was sort of an eerie cast on the beach. I don't know how to describe it. It just felt like impending doom.

The next morning at the store it was strange because no one was coming in. There were always people around in the mornings because I always had a pot of coffee going. I supplied free coffee. Many people started out their day with coffee at the store. We would talk about local politics and swap jokes. But there was hardly anybody coming in that day, and I didn't know what was going on. So when I took my lunch I walked to the ocean. I was standing on a hill, then I moved to another hill. I looked back to where I'd just come from, and the tide melted that hill just like sugar. You couldn't see into the ocean, it was so angry. It would rain a little while, snow a little while.

Then we found that all along the coast from New Jersey to Florida was washed out. The tide only trickled in to Corolla Village though. In Penny's Hill two elderly ladies died. One lady went out with her son to let the horse out of the stable and she couldn't get back. The other lady was about 87, she was at home and there was no way to get her out. The tide flooded her house and moved it 500 yards. The tide line was up to the ceiling.

Up to that point, all of my life we had never really had anything that really altered the beach dunes. Anytime I was going up the beach or coming home at night and wondered where I was, I could just shine the car lights on the dunes. I knew every dune just by the shape. I could always tell where I was. I gave out of gas one night, and I pulled up to a dune and I knew the Beasley family lived just behind it. So I went there and Mrs. Beasley siphoned some gas off for me to get home. Right now I wouldn't know where I was by the dunes, but back then all the hills kept their characteristics.

The day after the Ash Wednesday storm, right out here on the beach, there were clams, these big old sea clams. They were piled high. Also there were conch shells with the meat in them. The storm really emptied the ocean right up on the shore. I took a truckload of those clams to Virginia Beach and tried to sell them. People had never seen clams that big so they didn't want to try them. Finally this man who had a home on the Lynnhaven River gave me 5 cents a clam for the whole truckload.

We ate the clams and they were good. My mother took the meat out of the shells and put it in a meat grinder and ground it up. She made clam chowder that was delicious. It had potatoes and onions and the clams all ground up. The chowder was all substance. If you like clams it was pretty good.

When I was growing up, most anytime you had a real cold day and the wind blowing out of the west, you could go down to the beach and pick up clams, as many as you wanted. We'd get a lot of them. My mother would put them up in the freezer. Even today there are some people here who are real crafty and they know how to do it and they're out there on the cold days with a west wind.

After the Ash Wednesday storm I thought there wouldn't be anymore building on the oceanfront anymore. They had really developed the Sandbridge community on the oceanfront in Virginia Beach. There was one home in Sandbridge that had just been featured in American Home magazine. And you could pick up pieces of that house all up and down the beach in Corolla. It had a purple front on it, and it really scattered that far and near. But it wasn't but about three or four months until they started building again.

Corolla and Duck have always been pretty well protected from floods compared to other parts of the Outer Banks. The only time I ever heard of a flood was in 1933. There was a hurricane in July and one two weeks later in August. The water came down Jones's Hill Road and it flooded some of the houses on the west side of the road. I had an aunt who lived on the north end of the village and she had to be picked up by a life boat with her two baby sons. They all went to Corolla Island. Mr. and Mrs. Knight told them to go there.

A spring nor'easter drove the Cherokee *on the beach in Corolla in May 1956.*

In 1944 I was six years old. To me that was the worst hurricane I ever saw. Trees were knocked down. The Knapp House roof was torn up. There was a lot of damage in the village. Up until Isabel a few years ago that was the worst I'd seen. I remember one hurricane when my Daddy and I were at home alone. When the eye was passing over, it was real calm, and we were hearing all these birds. So we took a flashlight and went out in the yard. And there were little exotic birds sitting around in the trees, not anything we'd ever seen around here. When the wind got ready to shift again they went on. I guess they were trying to stay in the eye. I don't know where they came from, but they were tropical. Every tree was full of them. They blew in with the storm and moved on with the wind.

When I was growing up, we heard weather news on the radio. And people had an instinctive knowledge of the weather, older people especially. I heard them say that when a hurricane was

building up down south you'd hear the ocean make noises like a gunshot. They said if you have a sundog it indicates bad weather. A moondog meant the same thing. And if you count the stars between the ring around the moon and the moon, that told you how many days till bad weather. There were a lot of sayings that people depended on and they were pretty accurate.

We always followed this old Pamunkey Indian tale that when the moon was rising it was high tide, when the moon was overhead, like at 12 o'clock, it was low tide and when the the moon started going back down the water was coming back in. When it was all the way down it was high water again. Once I was in Virginia Beach with some friends and I saw that the moon was going down. I looked at the moon and said "Oh no! The moon is going down, I have to get home before high tide." The ride down the beach at high tide could take an hour or longer, but at low tide on the smooth sand it was only about 25 minutes. They'd never heard that saying and they all made fun of me for living by the moon and the tides.

Gates

When I was growing up, we always went north to Virginia to get anything, and we drove on the beach. Before they built the bridge at Kitty Hawk in the 1930s, even the people from Nags Head and Hatteras went all the way up north to Virginia on the beach. The Midgett brothers from Hatteras Island even started a bus service between Virginia and Hatteras Island.

In the early 1970s there was a lot of development starting here. And a scary thing happened. They made it so the residents of the Currituck Outer Banks were blocked from driving either to the north or the south. Some of the big-time developers saw a chance that they could isolate this area into an island of sorts and this would be more of an exotic area. They used a lot of influence to close off traffic in the Back Bay National Refuge, which meant you couldn't drive from Corolla to Virginia on the beach. At the end of Sandbridge is a 4-mile area of beach called Back Bay National Wildlife Refuge. Adjoining that on the south is False Cape State Park. When they started to close it off, we protested. If you counted Carova, we had about 100 people. Congress eventually said that those of us who had lived here and traveled that way for generations had prescriptive rights to travel as we always had. They gave us permits to drive through, but no one else could. Anyone who moved in after 1976 was not allowed to have a permit. At the time they issued permits there was about

50 of us who had them. Now there's only about 20 people who have a permit to go through. I still have my permit and can go to Virginia by driving up the beach. Actually I'm glad now that they blocked off the north end, because it would really be terrible if we had traffic coming in from Virginia Beach today.

At the same time they closed up the border on the north end, a developer closed off the road that we used on the south end at the Dare County line. There used to be a road where the Kitty Hawk Elementary School is; that road went through Duck Woods and came up here. It was called State Road 1152 in Currituck County. The state had always kept the road up. They hauled shells off the beach and put them on the road when I was growing up.

But then the state allowed the developers to close that road off at the Dare County line. You were not allowed to drive from Dare to Currituck County on that road unless you owned one of the developers' lots. They had a guard gate on the road and the guard stopped traffic. Well, the primary property owner said that the long-term residents of Corolla had a right to use the road without paying for anything. But I had just built my new building and moved JW Austin store there, and the guards jumped on me and said that my delivery trucks and gas trucks for the store couldn't have access through there. They threatened me, "Why don't you just buy a lot?" So I did.

The developers kept that road blocked for four or five years. It was a real frightening controversy. Imagine if you woke up one day and your road, either end of you, the way you travel, is blocked off with a guard gate. It somehow just seemed un-American. Both ends were blocked

Photo Courtesy: Norris Austin

Sheriff Griggs O'Neal and Norris at JW Austin Store.

at the same time. Can you imagine how frightening that was? To have people tell you when you can travel and what time? It felt like a foreign country.

Looking Back

I guess Corolla was really a good place to grow up. It was lonely at times because in my later years there weren't that many people my age around. I was about to get married once, but I guess when she figured out I was going to stay in Corolla she decided not to go through with it. I guess old age causes this, but it used to seem like the days back then were long, lazy and hazy. You had all day ahead of you to do what you wanted to. After you got off work you had a long time before sunset to do things. Now it seems like I get up and I turn around twice and the day is gone.

I'm kind of like an ostrich in the fact that I just stick my head in the sand and try not to look at the way it's changed. If I just go out on the main road it's not that bad. But when I get down to Pine Island it looks like row houses, like Long Island. I really do just try not to think about all the development. But when I go up in the lighthouse, I just can't believe how filled up it is. That's the reason I don't go up there any more than I have to.

I still live on the same land where I grew up. No one can imagine what this property means to me. I'm the third generation on this property. I've done a lot of visiting around the United States, and I've never seen any other place I would want to live. I can always take off my hearing aids and get in the garden and go back to like it was 40 years ago. 🐕

First, a few tips about the walking tour...

The Walking Tour route is a little over a mile long, taking you past all the remaining historic sites of Corolla. It starts at The Whalehead Club, then goes to the Currituck Beach Lighthouse and into the old village, with the vernacular architecture of village homes, an old schoolhouse and church, plus a few historic buildings that were moved into the village, like an historic Life-Saving Station. Along the way you'll walk down unpaved roads and along a wooden boardwalk over Currituck Sound.

Following the tour from point to point exactly as it's written will take less than an hour. However, you'll want to stop and tour The Whalehead Club and Currituck Beach Lighthouse, and we suggest that you stop along the way to browse in the shops, take a rest or have a bite to eat. We definitely recommend a visit to the Outer Banks Center for Wildlife Education, which is not a historic site but its exhibits have much to tell about the natural and cultural history of the Outer Banks. Before you know it, you will have spent a couple of hours exploring Corolla Village.

When you're on the tour, try for a little while to forget the modern world outside of this village. Stretch your imagination out to the time when the oceanfront was barren and the lighthouse was the only light seen for miles in any direction. Wrap your mind around the isolation of this village that felt like the end of the earth, separated from the world by miles of sand and water. Imagine the old village when it was made up of just a few buildings and homes along Corolla Village Road. The photographs that accompany the sites will help get an image of the village as it was.

But don't get completely lost in the past. Notice how the village buildings have been able to retain their former character while adapting to the modern world. The tour is meant to be done at a leisurely pace, so slow down and explore.

Keep in mind that several of the sites on the tour are private residences. Please respect private property. We sincerely request that you restrict your tour activities to walking in front of the building, pausing to read its history and then moving on without bothering its residents or entering the property, unless it is a public business.

THE COROLLA WALKING TOUR 🐎

1. Whalehead Club

When it was completed in 1925, this grand house was known as Corolla Island. Edward C. Knight Jr. and his wife, Marie Louise LeBel Knight, had the house built as a private home where they could enjoy leisure time and hunting on the Outer Banks. Edward Knight was a Philadelphia businessman and heir to a sugar fortune. Marie was a French Canadian socialite in Newport, Rhode Island. This was the second marriage for both, as their first spouses had died.

Edward Knight discovered the area in the late 1800s when he became a member of the Lighthouse Club of Currituck Sound, a hunting club located near the current Whalehead Club site. Knight bought the entire Lighthouse Club property in March of 1922 and that same year began construction on a stunning new house in the middle of the marsh near Corolla. The workers constructed the first floor, then dug a mote-like canal around the property and mounded the dredged material around the first floor to create the basement. (You can't put a basement underground on the island because the water table is so high.) In 1923, Knight changed the name of the club and property to Corolla Island, writing in his logbook: "The word "club" is misleading. We are building on a piece of land to the North of the present clubhouse, a substantial house which we shall occupy as our residence. We are also making a waterway around

Directions:
We begin and end our tour at the historic Whalehead Club, where plenty of parking is available.

Image Courtesy: Whalehead Preservation Trust

Mr. Edward Collings Knight Jr. No portraits or photographs of Mrs. Knight have been located.

The Whalehead Club in the 1940s with Corolla village in the background. The steeple of Corolla chapel can be seen directly above the Whalehead Club.

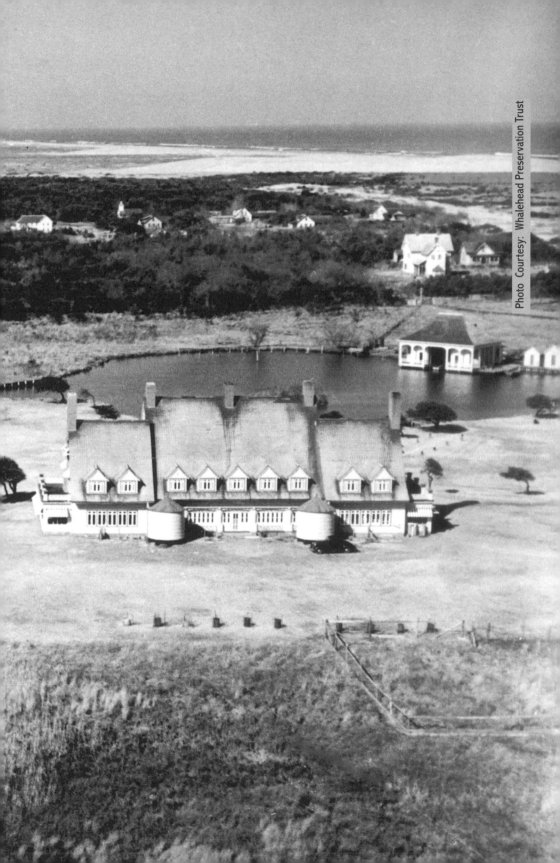

1948

Coast Palace In Carolina Houses Club

COROLLA, N. C.—One of the most unusual and palatial homes on the seacoast has rarely even been seen except by commercial fishermen bobbing around in Currituck sound, or by a handful of sportsmen who come here for the unexcelled waterfowling. And it cost its owner not a dime.

Sitting on this narrow and lonely sandbank, the Whalehead club is a mute monument to a plush era of splendid spending which Americans possibly will never see again. Built many years ago by Edward C. Knight Jr., it reputedly cost more than $360,000 and could not be duplicated now for perhaps three times that much, if at all. It was large enough to house 400 men during the war.

How It Was Built

Knight was an artist, and late in life married a young woman who also was an artist. Old-timers here say that sometimes the husband would build a part of the house which his artistic wife did not like, and she would rebuild it to suit her notions.

Its gabled roofs rise with magnificent serenity above a little island reached by a bridged moat, and the place seems incongruous among the shifting sand dunes, the rugged old Currituck light, and the hardy fishermen who set their carp nets in the shoaly waters near by.

Knight had a fancy for doors, and each room usually has three or four, leading helter-skelter into corridors. The couple also liked paintings (there were 63 of them), and among those remaining in the lodge is a self-portrait of the builder.

Log Records The Past

The club had a romantic history. Originally, there were some crude buildings on the property owned by a group of northern sportsmen who used them during the waterfowl season. The club would not permit women on the premises,

NEW YORK

---

this piece of land, thus forming an island."

The Corolla Island house was built between 1922 and 1925 for a price of $383,000. The architect is unknown at this time. Painted butter yellow, the mansion on the marsh must have been a grand sight to the modest-living locals, though it was not as lavish as the standards the Knights were used to. The house features five chimneys and a gable roof sheathed in gleaming copper, sweeping down to dormers and banks of windows that captured the stunning views of Currituck Sound and the surrounding landscape. Inside, the 23,000-square-foot house is outfitted with opulent Art Nouveau details, rich mahogany doors and curved trim, cork floors, Tiffany light fixtures and waterlily ornamentation. The house had things the local homes didn't have: an Otis elevator, generated electricity, steam radiators, fresh or salt running water, a grand piano and the 6,000-square-foot basement. The Knights built Corolla Island for private enjoyment; it has few public rooms while the living quarters and servants' quarters are extensive. The meticulously kept house logbook notes nearly forty different guests that visited Corolla to shoot during the fall and winter waterfowl hunting season. Recently discovered guest books show hundreds of visitors throughout the year, with one lady staying for eight months.

The Knights used the Corolla Island house from 1925 until 1934. In 1931, they painted the house a salmon color to match the boathouse, which was built in 1927. They left Corolla Island abruptly in November of 1934 and never returned. Both Knights died in 1936, within three months of each other. Since then the house has had many lives.

The house sat empty until 1940, when Ray T. Adams of Washington, D.C., reportedly bought it for only $25,000. Adams was the one to rename it the Whalehead Club, after a former moniker for the village of Corolla. Adams made some architectural changes and entertained there often, including many dignitaries from the capital. During World War II, Adams leased the club to the U.S. Coast Guard, who used it as a training facility. Adams died suddenly in the Whalehead Club on December 31, 1957.

In 1958, the building changed hands again, and from 1959 to 1961 it housed a summer school for boys called Corolla Academy. In 1963, the house became the home of Atlantic Research Company, which tested rocket fuel on the Banks. In the 1970s and '80s, the Whalehead Club sat empty. One developer after another made plans for the club as a resort, a hotel, a restaurant but nothing ever worked out. Over the course of years, someone painted the house and boathouse cream-colored.

In 1992 Currituck County bought the Whalehead Club, which was then dilapidated and crumbling after 20 years of neglect. The county spent nearly $5 million restoring the house and property. Today, the house looks exactly as it did when it was completed in 1925, when it was known as Corolla Island. The interior and exterior paints are the exact colors of the original, the architectural

Photo Courtesy: Whalehead Preservation Trust

Mr. Ray T. Adams (right) and Cornelius Midgett hunting in 1945.

elements are back in place and the copper roof and cork floors have been replaced. Furnishings taken from the house over the years are slowly coming back in. Guided tours of the house and its historic significance are offered. See our Attractions chapter.

Directions:
From the front (south) door of the Whalehead Club, look out toward the sound at the strip of land that juts into the sound.

2. Former Airstrip

If you look at the sound shore on the backside of the clubhouse, you'll see a point of land that juts into the sound and stacks of eroded pilings sticking out of the water. When Ray Adams owned the Whalehead Club, this point of land was much longer. In the early 1950s, before the little soundside pond was dug, Adams had an airstrip constructed on the front lawn. He bulk-headed the point of land to protect it from erosion and landed planes on the grass. Atlantic Research, which owned the building in later years, used the airstrip often. Shirley Austin, who worked with Atlantic Research and often flew off-island with the pilot to buy groceries, remembers having to run out to the airstrip to chase away grazing cows so planes could land. The point of

Photo Courtesy: Norris Austin

This aerial view of the Whalehead Club shows a clear view of the airstrip.

land and the bulkhead eroded away a great deal, leaving the bare points of the pilings exposed in the sound.

3. Bridge

Part of the Corolla Island ensemble included two ornate bridges. Before constructing the house, the Knights dug canals around the property and used the extracted material to provide high ground on which to build. Workers built two decorative and functional bridges to span the canals. This is one of the two original bridges, built in 1922. The other bridge was at the current paved entrance to the parking lot. No doubt the Knights, their servants and guests drove their Model A cars across the bridges when visiting their residence. When traveling to Corolla from Philadelphia or Rhode Island, the Knights would take the train to Norfolk then drive Model As all the way down the beach from Virginia. Locals call the water

Directions:
When leaving the Whalehead Club from the tour exit or Museum Shop, walk across the parking lot and lawn. Head to the left, toward the humpback bridge spanning a small canal.

Photo Courtesy: Whalehead Preservation Trust

under this bridge The Ditch and say it's a good little fishing hole.

*The Whalehead Club
boat heading out with guests.*

Directions:

After crossing the bridge, head out to the scenic gazebo then take a right and walk along the sidewalk next to the boat basin toward the pinkish-colored boathouse.

4. Boathouse

The small salmon-colored boathouse was built in 1927, two years after the Corolla Island house was completed. The boathouse has the same architectural details as the house, but it was painted pink, a strange complement to the bright yellow house. The color on the boathouse today is an exact reproduction of the original pink color. Mrs. Knight must have been happy with the color choice, for in 1931 she painted the entire house pink to match the boathouse.

The boathouse was used to store hunting skiffs and hunting supplies. It also housed a grain elevator and chutes, a warehouse, generators for supplying the house with electricity and an office. Back in the days before federal hunting regulation, the hunting guides fed and baited the waterfowl on a regular basis, so storage of grain was an issue. The boathouse cantilevers over the water so that boats can drive right into the house for lift-out and storage. Pulleys hoisted boats out of the water for dry storage. On one wall were vertical metal pipes used to hang the waterfowl to cure.

5. Currituck Beach Lighthouse

In the late 19th century, the U.S. Lighthouse Board built a string of brick, first-order lighthouses on the coast of North Carolina to warn mariners off the shores of the Banks and to help them identify their locations. These lighthouses were much more grand and useful than the ones previously built along the Banks. The Currituck Beach Lighthouse, 34 miles south of Cape Henry [Virginia] Lighthouse and 32.5 miles north of Bodie Island Lighthouse, was the last of the great brick lighthouses built on the Outer Banks, approved by Congress in 1872 "to illuminate the dark space . . . between Body's island and Cape Henry." It cost $50,000 to construct the tower between 1873-75.

The Currituck Beach Lighthouse follows the standard conical design of other lighthouses of its period, with stone trim, elegant ironwork and a glass cap. The conical shape, steadily narrowing to the top, was achieved by varying the number of bricks in the width of the tower walls and also by tapering the thickness of the interior walls. At the base, the walls are five feet eight inches thick and the top is three feet thick. In all, the highly skilled masons laid one million bricks in the tower. The lighthouse was left unpainted, so its natural, rich, red-brick color is its distinguishing daymark. Its night beacon was originally five seconds on, 90 seconds off, but today its flash cycle is 3 seconds on, 17 seconds off. At the base of the tower is the small oil house/work vestibule with two corbelled chimneys and kingpost gabled decorations. Inside, ten curved flights of iron stairs 214 steps in all lead to the top of the tower.

Directions:
Follow the footpath to the left, in the direction of the lighthouse. Once you reach the road, turn right. Cut through the wooded area to the two board-and-batten buildings that contain restrooms. Go between the two restroom buildings and straight across you'll see the lighthouse entrance. In season, there's an ice cream and refreshment stand outside the lighthouse entrance.

PhotoCourtesy: Outer Banks Conservationists

The Currituck Beach Lighthouse compond forms a neat quadrangle of historic sites. Our first stop in the compound is the lighthouse itself. If you have to wait in line to climb, you can view and read about other sites as you wait. The lighthouse in open to climbing from Easter to Thanksgiving only (see the Attractions chapter for other details). All of the sites in the quadrangle are connected by a circular brick path.

Directions:
West of the lighthouse, directly across the lawn, is the Double Light Keepers' House. This site is not open to the public except on special occasions.

The Currituck Beach Lighthouse was lit on December 1, 1875. Its first-order designation stems from the size of its lens. First-order lighthouses used the largest and highest-powered of the seven Fresnel lenses available. The original source of light in the lens was a mineral-oil lamp consisting of five wicks, the largest of which was four inches in diameter. The lens was rotated by a mechanical device, giving it the illusion of flashing. The keeper had to crank the device every two and a half hours to keep it rotating. The hard-working keepers also had to clean the lens and windows, trim the wicks and fuel the lamps, in addition to maintaining the lighthouse buildings and grounds and providing food for their families. With the advent of electricity, the lighthouse was automated in 1939.

6. Double Light Keepers' House

This large Victorian Stick style dwelling was a standard issue of the U.S. Lighthouse Board. It was built according to the plans for a "Keepers Dwelling for a First Order Lighthouse," designed by government-hired professional architects during Reconstruction. These designs were inspired by the work of A. J. Downing, who brought the Carpenter Gothic movement to mainstream America.

The keepers' house was prefabricated, right down to the weatherboarded siding, decorative battens, finials, crossbar, kingpost ornament and porcelain doorknobs. The house was sent to the Currituck Beach location by barge, and the pre-cut and labeled materials were assembled on site on 1876. An inscription in the attic indicates that W. C. Horner, a German house builder from Baltimore, finished constructing the house on May 8, 1876. The Currituck Beach Keepers' House was one of the most decorative of all keepers' houses built under the First Order Lighthouse Dwelling Plans. The same plan was also used at Morris Island and Hunting Island in

South Carolina, but neither of those buildings has survived.

The house was built as a duplex, each side a mirror image of the other, one for each light keeper and his family. There are two front doors, two separate front porches and two back doors. The most interesting divisive technique is the separation of the paths leading to the front and back of the house. There are two identical brick walkways, one for each keeper, running side by side. At one time a fence separated these narrow paths, so that for one keeper to get to the other side of the house, he had to go all the way down to the street and walk up his neighbor's path.

On either side of the house, each family had two louvered cisterns that were fed rainwater by gutters, an outhouse and a storage building. At one point, before the Little Keeper's House was moved onsite, there were three keepers sharing this duplex. The principal keeper lived

The Currituck Beach Lighthouse compound in the late 1890s.

Bamber Photo Courtesy: Outer Banks Conservationists

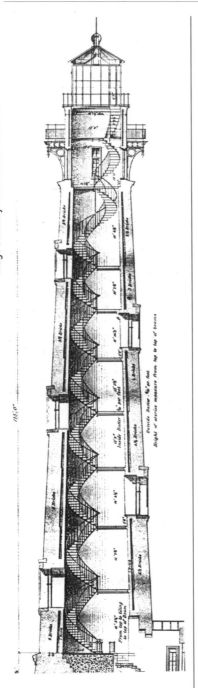

The original plan for the Currituck Beach Lighthouse.

on the south end of the house with his family, while the two assistant keepers and their families had to share the north end. The north-end cistern was expanded to accommodate the extra people. The light keepers' wives were expected to keep the houses clean and were even graded in housekeeping at random inspections. The inspectors were even known to look in drawers and closets. One keeper was reportedly dismissed for his wife's poor housekeeping skills.

When the lighthouse was automated in 1939 the Keepers' House was no longer needed. For a long time the house was used for hay and horse feed storage for the Coast Guards horses that lived in stables behind the Little Keepers' House. Tourists and visitors who discovered the house helped themselves to doors and windows, moldings and other interior elements, while men from the Navy station were accused of taking all the brass to sell for quick cash. By 1970 the Keepers' House was weathered, dilapidated and overgrown with vines, but its roof and interior were strangely intact. The restorers say that the salt air blowing through the empty window and doorframes must have preserved the interior boards. In 1980 a nonprofit group known as Outer Banks Conservationists leased the Keepers' House from the state and began restoring it. Since the government plans for a Keepers' Dwelling for a First Order Lighthouse were still available in historic archives, it was possible for OBC to reproduce the house almost exactly as it was. An interior doorway now connects the two sides on the lower level, but the middle floor is still divided. The original heart-pine floors, chimneys, fireplace and many other original elements are still intact. The house is opened to the public for tours once a year (see the Attractions chapter for details).

Bamber Photo Courtesy: Outer Banks Conservationists

210. C. S. 6. CURRITUCK BEACH LT. STA., N. C.

The Storehouse Privy in the 1890s.

7. Storehouse Privy

On the south end of the compound quadrangle, this small, white board-and-batten building, with four sharp finials to match the Keepers' House, was at one time a kitchen and also a storage building for the light keepers' equipment. In the 1970s the Coast Guard almost destroyed this building because it sat in the right-of-way of the road that runs right by here. Just as they were about to burn it down, Corolla resident Norris Austin offered to move it. Austin made a great effort to remove the building from its foundation and move it down the road to the village. Later, Outer Banks Conservationists bought the building and moved it back to its original footprint. They restored it to its former appearance and converted it into an office for the light keeper and lighthouse staff.

Isn't it interesting that all of the lighthouse compound buildings, even the privies, are

Directions:
To the south (right) of the lighthouse is an outbuilding.

Directions:

North of the lighthouse, to the left if you're facing the lighthouse entrance, is the Privy and Little Light Keeper's House.

The privy before it was returned to its original state.

Photo Credit: M. Parker

architecturally interesting and well constructed? All of the buildings are not only useful but also decorative, proving that the U.S. Lighthouse Board took pride in the appearance of its sites.

8. Privy

Here is a good place to pause and feel grateful for the wonders of modern plumbing. Next to the Little Keeper's House is the original two-seater privy, restored to give modern-day visitors an idea of the lifestyle of the former keepers. With its clapboard walls and beaded wood on the inside, even the privy is picturesque, carrying through the fine Victorian style of the other compound buildings. The privy was restored in 1994. A clear plastic door allows a rare view of the intricacies — or lack thereof — of old-time plumbing.

9. Little Light Keeper's House (Lighthouse Museum Shop)

When the U.S. Lighthouse Board established a third light keeper position at Currituck Beach, it was a great help to the two keepers. But since the Keepers' House was designed for two families only, the third keeper and his family had to move into the north-end duplex with the assistant keeper while the principal keeper lived on the south end. This couldn't have been a pleasant situation.

Relief came about 1920 with the move of this building from Coinjock on the mainland to the lighthouse compound on the Outer Banks. Presumably built around 1874, the building was originally the residence at Long Point Depot, which was a federal transfer point for lighthouse and lighted buoy materials. Built in the Victorian Stick style, it is similar in style to the large Keepers' House. It was floated by barge across the sound to this point in 1920. The primary keeper moved into this home and the two assistant keepers lived on either side of the double keepers' quarters. A cement cistern was built on the east side to catch rainwater for the main keeper.

With the help of the third man, the lighthouse keepers were able to do their regular duties as well as assist with a round-the-clock watch for World War I activity off the coast. During World War II when the Coast Guard had a station at Corolla, the cottage was used for hay storage for the horses that lived in stable just behind here. After that the building sat empty and was so overgrown with vines and briars that most people didn't even realize it existed. Its rotting and weathered wood was all but invisible under the dense, twisting growth. In 1985 Outer Banks Conservationists began to protect and restore the remains of the building. The house was restored with many of the original materials. In the interior upstairs it's easy to distinguish the old materials from the new. In 1995 OBC opened it as the Lighthouse Museum Shop, and visitors are welcome inside.

Photo Credit: M. Parker

Compare this view of the Little Keeper's House before restoration with the current building, and you will begin to appreciate the incredible work done by Outer Banks Conservationists.

A view of the Little Keeper's House looking west in the 1890s.

Bamber Photo Courtesy: Outer Banks Conservationists

Directions:

When leaving the Museum Shop, exit to the right and walk behind the shop and go through the yard and through the wooden gate. Walk past the storage building, down the driveway and turn right on the paved road..

10. Corolla Village Road

Here is a good place to imagine what Corolla was like long ago. In the late 1800s and early 1900s, the road was, of course, unpaved. In the early days, there was much less vegetation along this stretch of Corolla Village Road, and the Currituck Sound would have been visible from where you now walk. In the early 20th century, Corolla Village Road connected the Coast Guard station, Corolla Island, the lighthouse and the docks with the village, then extended beyond the village about 9 miles up to Wash Woods. In the '50s when Corolla got electricity, this road also connected the village to the Pole Road, along which ran the utility poles, parallel to the beach.

Imagine the villagers riding their horses or walking down this dirt path to meet visitors coming over on the mailboat or to meet a boat for a journey across the sound. Imagine the light keepers and their families using this road to travel to and from school, church and the general store. In later years, the state maintained the road by paving it with seashells taken from the beach. Imagine the schoolchildren walking along the hard-packed shells from the schoolhouse to the public docks.

Directions:

Walk to the corner of Corolla Village Road and Schoolhouse Road.

11. Corolla School

Corolla Village Road and Schoolhouse Road

No one knows exactly when this front-gable frame schoolhouse was built. Some people put the date at 1905, though others believe it was built even before that. Corolla native Norris Austin believes his father and uncles were attending the school as early as 1896. Two Corolla citizens, Sol Sanderlin and Val Twiford, are credited with its construction. The builders used salvaged materials and even a ship's timber in constructing the schoolhouse, a testament to the resourcefulness of the isolated Outer Bankers. The schoolhouse looked then very much the way it looks today — a louvered belfry at its front gable, white weatherboarded exterior, a chimney and two frame privies out back. The small board-and-batten rear extension was added later, to accommodate a lunchroom and more students.

Before the school opened, there were several small schools in Corolla. There was one school for the children of government employees at the lighthouse and life-saving station, another for the children of the local fishermen and yet another for the children who lived in the village. The village parents paid for the individual schools, but in 1905 the Currituck County School System created a unified Corolla School, providing a teacher, textbooks and standardized grading. Children of all grades went to the school, and children from nearby villages were bused to the school in later years. Norris Austin remembers that in his first year of school, in 1944, there were 60 children attending this school. By the next year, however, those numbers had dropped off as families moved out of Corolla after the war. One teacher had the responsibility of teaching all grades levels from first to twelfth grade, which might explain why students remember getting a new teacher almost every year. The schoolhouse was the center of the community, and dances, concerts, plays, cakewalks and village meetings were held within its walls. The children held plays, carnivals and dances to raise money for their library books and sports equipment.

In the 1950s the population of Corolla began to dwindle. Where once there were many as 50 students at the school, in 1955 there were only five students enrolled. In 1958 Currituck County closed the school. The Board of Education minutes noted: "The State Board of Education did not

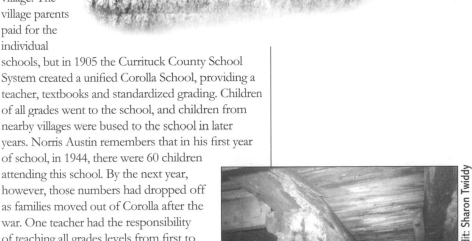

A view of one of the salvaged ship's timbers used in construction of the schoolhouse.

School children at the Corolla School around the turn of the last century.

allot a teacher for Corolla. The board stated that the parents of the two children in attendance be informed of this." For a couple of years after the closing, the Corolla Academy, a summer boys school at the Whalehead Club, used the Corolla school as a recreation hall, with a pool table set up in the main room. In later years the house was a residence. In 1999 a local preservationist had the school restored. During the restoration workers found, bchind thc walls and undcr the floors, old Valentines, pencil nubs, a sheet of schoolwork dated 1906, a library book overdue since 1927 and a seven-for-one-cent candy wrapper.

This summer, Twiddy and Company, the current owners of the schoolhouse, will have it open to the public for the first time in many years. Current plans are for a display on the wild horses.

Directions:

Keep walking down Corolla Village Road; diagonally across the corner from the schoolhouse is the next site.

Featured Shopping:
• Spry Creek Dry Goods..... page 135

12. Hayman-Austin-Scarborough Residence

1122 Corolla Village Road

This home was one of the largest residences in Corolla village, and it is the one of oldest that remains standing today. Henry Hayman built this two-story side-gable dwelling at the turn of the 20th century, sheathing it in weatherboard siding like the rest of the village buildings. In 1917 the house was given to Hayman's granddaughter, Lela, who grew up in down the road and married Pell Austin, son of light keeper William Riley Austin. Pell joined the U.S. Coast Guard in 1917 and served for 30 years. Lela and Pell had 11 children, eight sons and three daughters, and they found it necessary to add on the house. Pell added an ell to the back, with a gable-on-hip roof that was reminiscent of Coast Guard building styles. The family used the upstairs portion of the addition as sleeping quarters for the three girls. Lela and Pell's son, Gene, lives in Corolla today.

Some of the original features of the house are intact the back hip roof porch, with its original molded weatherboard siding, turned post supports and millwork porch rail and two-over-two double-hung sash windows.

Jewell and Jim Scarborough of Nags Head bought the house in 1959 to use as a vacation residence. They bought the house sight-unseen for $3,000, at the suggestion of their friends Helen and Elwood Parker,

The Scarboroughs in the back of their house in the 1970s.

who owned the house across the street. Several families would visit the house together, the men hunting and fishing and the children playing in the practically empty village and going down to John Austin's post office and store for a Coke. Mrs. Scarborough remembers that back in those days wild pigs ran loose all around Corolla, and the menfolk would catch them to have barbecues on the beach. The children remember having to scamper up into trees to get away the wild pigs.

Overzealous shoppers have been known to walk in the front door of this private residence, but don't make that mistake yourself. It's a private residence, still in the Scarborough family.

Directions:
About 150 feet down the road on your left look for the white house with a porch tucked under the green roof. This house is now Outer Banks Style, a retail store that you are welcome to enter.

Featured Shopping:

13. Gray-Lewark House
1130 Corolla Village Road

Curtis and Blanche Gray had this charming house built before 1918, some say as early as 1896. It is said that Mrs. Gray, who was the teacher at Corolla school for a time, designed the house herself. But historians believe it is more likely that Mrs. Gray got the plans for the house from a catalog of house designs, as was a popular custom in the early 20th century. Mr. Gray was Corolla's merchant, grocer and postmaster, and his store was next door to his house, probably on the same footprint as the bookstore building is today. (The store building was later moved, and then burned.) Mrs. Gray fell ill with influenza and died soon after they moved in. Mr. Gray, it's said, then swapped his house and post office with the house of Harold Hampton of Waterlily and moved to the mainland. It is reported that the ghostly presence remains in an upstairs room, infusing it with a warm and fuzzy feeling. Go upstairs to the blue room to see for yourself, as today this building is a retail shop.

Humphrey and Gertie Lewark bought the house from Mr. Hampton and raised three children there. One of the Lewark daughters, Odessa, inherited the house and eventually left it to her son, William Griggs. Another Lewark daughter, Helen, inherited another family home, the Parker House (site 18).

This was an unusual house for the village. It is Corolla's only example of an early Colonial Revival frame bungalow, with Neoclassical Revival and Craftsman style exterior elements. Its original molded weatherboarding is intact on the main part of the house, and the one-story rear ell has its original german siding. The kitchen and dining room were added on in 1925, and you can see the siding of the original house in that room. The intriguing front dormer balcony has its original hexagonal gable shingles, plain rail balustrade and weatherboarded "cheeks," which

Photo Courtesy: Norris Austin

served as a wind buffer. Note the fact that there is no door to the balcony. To use the balcony, the residents would have had to crawl out a window. Inside, the house has some of its original features, including beaded board ceilings and walls and simple door and window surrounds. The interior wood and trim appears to be salvaged from other buildings because not all of it matches. When the building was being renovated into a retail shop in the 1990s, the renovators were given old beaded board wall covering from a mainland house that was about to be burned down. This wood was incorporated in with the original elements, carrying on the village tradition of using salvaged supplies wherever possible.

Corolla Village taken from the top of the lighthouse around 1929. Many of the buildings can be seen today in their original locations.

The numbers above correspond to locations on the walking tour:

11) Corolla Schoolhouse
12) Scarborough house
13) Gray-Lewark house
15) Corolla chapel
17) Austin house
19) Parker house

Directions:

Walk between the Lewark-Gray House and the bookstore and you'll see a small, white building out back. This is now a photography studio and gallery, which you are welcome to enter.

Lorenz Fine Photography, before restoration.

Photo Credit: Sharon Twiddy

14. Outbuilding of the Gray- Lewark House

1130 Corolla Village Road

This small building, today a retail shop, was once the outbuilding for the Gray-Lewark home. Mr. Lewark built the building and used the lower level as a workshop and the upper level to store hunting accoutrements and decoys. The building fits in with the style of the other buildings of the village because of its window trim, roof pitch and board-and-batten exterior. During restoration, old Currituck decoys were found in the attic. No romantic story here: It was just a storage building, though a quaint-looking one.

15. Corolla Chapel

1136 Corolla Village Road

The small front portion of this chapel is the historic portion of the building. For nearly 115 years the small chapel sat on the lot across the road, but it was moved in 2002 and attached to this larger building to accommodate growing congregations. It suits Corolla to move buildings around this way, as moving things around the village has been a common practice for more than a century.

The chapel was built in 1885, reportedly by the same two men who built the school — Sol Sanderlin and Val Twiford. The Corolla locals — both Baptists and Methodists — banded together to build the chapel, but it was known from the start as the Whaleshead Baptist Church.

Directions:

From Site 14 Walk north towards Corlla Chapel and towards the road. You'll pass by Outer Banks Style on your right.

Photo Credit: Eunice G. Overman

Inside the Corolla chapel.

(Whaleshead was one of the original names of this village.) The Methodists of the village soon left to form their own church six miles up the beach at Pennys Hill. The congregation of the Whaleshead Baptist Church was too small to support a resident preacher, so a preacher from the mainland visited only once a month, giving long Saturday and Sunday services to last out the month. Baptists from villages all along the northern Outer Banks, from Wash Woods and Duck, traveled to Corolla to attend these services.

In 1938, the Baptists dropped Corolla from their circuit, claiming it was too remote. However, the attendance records from that time period show that between 70 and 90 people were showing up at the services every Sunday. After that, the local residents continued to operate the chapel as a nondenominational house of worship.

If ever a preacher was visiting the area, someone would hang a sign in Johnny Austin's general store about upcoming services, and people would come from miles around to hear him speak. During World War II, the Protestants shared their small chapel with Catholic servicemen stationed at the Corolla Coast Guard base. In the 1960s and '70s, as Corolla's population reached its all-time low, the church wasn't used at all. However, John and Virginia Austin maintained and cleaned it so that it was always ready for the occasional minister who would come to town and hold Sunday services.

Since 1987 the Corolla Chapel has been an interdenominational house of worship under leadership of Pastor Strauss. Since 1992, the chapel has shared its space with the Catholic church for Wednesday night masses.

The plain frame, front-gable building with a small louvered belfry and three-sided apse is quite similar to the design of the school. The beaded pine walls and ceilings in the chapel were laid out in a herringbone style. Every year, the congregation put a light brushing of linseed oil on the walls and ceilings, which caused the pine to darken considerably over time. The original walls are still intact in the old portion of the chapel, but the ceiling was replaced with plaster. The original pulpit is still in the chapel, as is a wooden inlaid cross made by one of the local residents in 1885. When the chapel was moved across the street, the congregation took care to save its lines when meshing the old with the new. If you're curious about the chapel, attend a service on Sunday morning or Wednesday evening. You may catch the doors open during other times, especially on Wednesdays. As you walk along the tour, check the door to see if it's open so you can take a quick peek.

16. Lewark-Austin House

1208 Corolla Village Road, end of the road

At the end of the road on the northwest corner of the cul-de-sac, you'll see the cozy-looking home Corolla native Ottley Austin and his wife, Mazie. This 1920s Craftsman bungalow was originally the home of Cleveland and Grace Lewark. Cleveland was the caretaker at the Lighthouse Club and then the superintendent at Corolla Island for a number of years. The Lewarks used this house for a time as the Lighthouse View Hunt Club, accommodating waterfowl hunters who came to the area to shoot over the sound. Later the house was owned by postmaster Norris Austin, who traded it with his brother Ottley for the Austin House (site 17), which was closer to the post office.

This bungalow has a rear ell that was attached in later years. With exposed knee braces and a full-façade front shed porch, it is a well-preserved example of the simple dwellings of the early 20th-century residents of the Currituck Outer Banks. This is a private residence so please do not enter the yard.

The house to the east of this one is the 1920s Valentina Twiford home. Twiford was a builder who is credited with the construction of the schoolhouse and chapel. The Craftsman bungalow has rear ell kitchen that is not attached to the house. This is also private property so please do not enter the yard.

In days gone by, the road you stand on now extended 9 miles past this point, all the way up to Wash Woods. Just north of what is now this cul-de-sac was an area called Theodore's Landing. Here you would have found the first post office at Emma Parker's store, a blacksmith's shop, the original location of the Parker House (see site 18) and other homes.

Directions:

If you're feeling energetic, turn left and walk down to the cul-de-sac at the end of Corolla Village Road (about .02 of a mile) for a look at an especially quiet part of Corolla. If you'd rather save time, turn right here and walk back down Corolla Village. Skip over to the text for Site 17.

Photo courtesy: Whalehead Preservation Trust

Cleveland Lewark, caretaker of the Lighthouse Club and later superintendent of Corolla Island (the Whalehead Club).

Featured Shopping:
• The Village Fisherman.... page 136

Directions:
Walk back down Corolla Village Road to Site 17. With your back to the Island Bookstore, look directly across to the white house down the lane. This is a private residence so please do not enter the yard.

Photo Courtesy: Outer Banks Conservationists

William Riley & Lovie Austin

Directions:
Continue down Corolla Village Road to the white house on the corner. This house is now the Lighthouse Garden shop, and you are welcome to go inside.

FeaturedShopping:
•Lighthouse Garden Shop.. page 134

17. Austin House

The main body of the Austin House, set a ways off the road, was built in 1896 by Wallace O'Neal. William Riley Austin bought the house and moved in after he finished his tenure as light keeper in the 1920s. Austin later moved a cookhouse from a property near the lighthouse and connected it to this home. He tended a bountiful garden on the property in his retirement years. Austin's son, John, and his family lived in the house with the elder Austins until they passed away. John ran the local general store and post office (see site 20), which is located next to this house. John's children grew up in this house as well. Members of the family still live in the house today, marking the fifth generation of Austins in the Austin house. Please do not enter the yard of this private home.

18. Parker House (Lighthouse Garden)

1129 Corolla Village Road

This one-and-a-half story, side-gable house was constructed in the early 1900s. Its exterior details, such as the shaped rafter ends on the eaves and the german siding, came before the Craftsman style, which was so popular on the Banks after 1920. Walter Parker built the house just north of here, next door to the Lewark-Austin House (site 16). It was rolled on logs to this location in the 1920s. A one-story rear ell and breezeway were added, as was the front shed dormer. Note how the concrete for the foundation and steps are made from beach sand and shells, typical of the locals' creativity with available resources. Walter Parker sold the house to Humphrey Lewark, who owned the Gray-Lewark House (site 13). Mr. Lewark left the house to his daughter, Helen, who coincidentally had married Elwood Parker, bringing the home back into its original family.

This was Elwood and Helen's house for most of its life. The Parkers lived down the Banks but continued to use this house as a vacation home. The house was converted to a retail shop in the late 1990s. Most of the original beaded board wall covering is intact. If you go inside, you'll see many of the old doors and windows used as display tables. Former family members who have visited the house say that they never used the upstairs as living space, but rather to store their decoys. The little building behind this house, now Corolla Village Barbecue, was the garage and outbuilding for the Parker House.

Photo Credit: Sharon Twiddy

Notice how the original boards on the roof of the Parker house are different sizes, a clear sign that they were scavenged from the beach.

19. <u>Village Garden</u>

In the early days, the villagers raised their own food or caught it in the sea or shot it out of the sky. Everyone had a vegetable garden and fruit trees to provide fresh produce, and everything was canned and preserved to save for the stark winter months. Because Corolla village was on the more-protected sound side of the island, the gardens and plants were shielded from the lethal salt-laden winds of the ocean side. And the area's mild climate made for a long growing season. Longtime Corolla resident Shirley Austin especially remembers a village garden where one December she picked nine different vegetables for a salad.

Directions:
Walk between the Lighthouse Garden and its neighboring shop, Corolla Trading Company, to get to the garden.

The Village Garden is a reminder of these old sustenance gardens and the types of plants they bore. Most all the seeds grown here, mainly those in the vegetable garden, were available to Corollans during the period from 1900 to 1920. The gardener plants older and heirloom varieties, some of which are nearly extinct. Ever heard of cardoon? How about feverfew, Kellogg's Breakfast tomatoes, red burgundy okra or West Indian Gherkin cucumbers? These are just a few of the plants growing here that seem unusual to us but would have been common to Corolla village gardens. The gardener even grows indigo, which would have been used as a dye. Older varieties of roses and other native plants grow here as well. (See our Attractions chapter for more information.)

Directions:

Just beside the public garden, note the long white and green building in a yard behind the fence.

20. Old Corolla Post Office

The Corolla Post Office was established in 1895, with Emma Parker, who ran a local general store, as postmaster. That first post office was down at what is now the end of Corolla Village Road, but it moved several times as the postmaster's position changed hands in the years to

The post office (right) in the 1920s. At this time it was located up the road and was an ice cream store

follow. The building you are looking at now housed the post office for the longest period of time.

This little building was constructed by John

Photo Credit: Norris Ausitn

Austin in the 1920s
when the Knights were
building Corolla Island.
John, a native Corollan,
built the store right on
Corolla Village Road
and operated it with the
help of his sister. The
two made homemade ice
cream and sold it to the
Corolla Island workers.
Later they expanded
the store and sold dry
goods, groceries and
gas. In 1935, John was
appointed postmaster
and opened the post
office in the store. He
then decided to move
the store/post office
back off the road to
this location so it would
be closer to his house
(site 17). During World
War II, John Austin's
store was the PX for the
servicemen stationed at Corolla. Norris Austin,
John's son, remembers the servicemen lined up
all the way through the village waiting for their
candy and supplies. So much mail came in for the
servicemen that John would have to close the store
to sort the mail. In the 1950s, John added a parallel
extension at the north end of the building to make
room for more mailboxes. John was a dapper-
dressing, good-natured man who had a keen
recollection of all the events that had happened in
Corolla throughout his lifetime, and he was well
known for his stories. The general store and post
office was the hub of the small community, where
everyone gathered to talk about the weather, each
other and whatever else was going on.

    John served as postmaster until 1959, when
his son, Norris, took over the job. In 1981 Norris

*John Austin in front of the Corolla
Post Office, where he served as post
master for 24 years.*

Directions:
Leave the garden from the back entrance and walk in the direction of the playground/parking lot. The next site is behind the playground.

needed more room so he built a new post office, modeling his new building after the original village post office at Emma Parker's store. The post office remains in the Austin Building on Highway 12 today. This building was left just as it was, with the boxes and old pull-down iron-bar window, which are still inside. (Now the building is a private office.) Norris served as postmaster until 1992, ending the 57-year Austin-family postmaster regime. The Corolla Post Office must be a good place to work, because in 108 years of operation there have only been seven postmasters.

21. Kill Devil Hills Life Saving Station

Corner of Highway 12 and Schoolhouse Road

This building is not indigenous to Corolla village. Where it now sits was once dense vegetation. It was constructed at Kill Devil Hills in 1878, just east of the current Wright Brothers National Memorial, 20 miles south of Corolla. In the 1980s this historic treasure was crowded among motels, painted pink inside and used to house summer employees. Local real estate developer Doug Twiddy had it moved to Corolla in 1986, painstakingly restored it to historic codes and opened it as his real estate office. Now it is private business office. The station is relevant to Corolla's history, however, because the Life Saving Service played a large part in the village culture.

The Life Saving stations dotting the Outer Banks provided a crucial service to late 18th and early 19th century maritime traffic off the dangerous barrier island shores. The surfmen, as the lifesavers were called, patrolled the beach on horseback looking for ships in trouble and performed harrowing rescues on shipwrecks. The Chandler-style Currituck Beach Life-Saving Station was one of the first seven stations established along the Outer Banks in 1874 (11 more stations were established in 1878). The station was situated near the ocean, east of the Currituck Beach Lighthouse. Its original name was Jones Hill and it was also known as Whales Head at one point. The first building was replaced in 1903 with a Quonochontaug-type building. The original building was moved and then torn down in 1959. The 1903 building was moved approximately 6 miles north and placed on a site about 1,000 feet west of the original Penny's Hill Station. It is now a private residence. It is visible from the beach if you're driving up in the four-wheel-drive area north of Corolla.

The Kill Devil Hills Life-Saving Station has many of its original exterior and interior elements. The front-gable, one-and-a-half story frame building combines elements of Carpenter Gothic and Eastlake style. The original shingles are still on the exterior. The side shed extension, where lifesavers kept their gear, was added on at the turn of the century. Inside, the old station sign still hangs, and the building it looks like it did in the old days: unpainted tongue-and-groove pine on the walls and ceilings, and plain window and door surrounds

Photo Courtesy: Library of Congress

Surfmen pose at the Kill Devil Hills station in the early 1900s.

with bull's eye corner blocks.

The surfmen at the Kill Devil Hills Life-Saving Station were directly involved with Wilbur and Orville Wright and their experiments with flight at Kill Devil Hill. The Wright brothers' camp was near the station, and the surfmen helped them with their daily experiments. On December 17, 1903, three of the surfmen aided and witnessed the first flight, and one of them took the famous picture of that flight that we still see today.

Photo Courtesy: Norris Austin

Knapp House Road

Schoolhouse Road runs here now.

Directions:
At the corner, turn right and walk down Schoolhouse Road.

22. Schoolhouse Road

Schoolhouse Road was not a part of the original Corolla village, nor was, of course, N.C. Highway 12. This area between Corolla Village Road and the beach was just a stretch of natural vegetation until the 1970s, when developers cleared it to make this road. There was, however, a sand road that ran parallel to where this one is now. Called Knapp House Road, it branched off from Corolla Village Road and ran between the post office and the Parker House (right where the Village Garden is now) out to the beach. The road led out to Mr. Knapp's house, the first oceanfront dwelling in the area. Along Knapp House Road, about where the playground is now, was a large, imposing, late-1800s home that originally belonged to the Hayman family. The house changed hands many times and at one point was known as the Sir Thomas Lodge. It was later torn down.

Next to the school, where Schoolhouse Road now lies, was where the children's playground and ball field were located. Even though there weren't enough children in the village to have organized team sports, the kids played games like volleyball and softball and Annie Over, says Norris Austin, who attended the school.

23. Gene and Shirley Austin House

8 Schoolhouse Road

This modest, one-story house was originally a barracks house and workstation for the Navy, which had a Loran station on the Currituck Beach Lighthouse compound, right next to the lighthouse. The building was built in 1957 and housed about five or six Navy personnel that were stationed at this lonely outpost. The Navy only used the building for a couple of years, then turned it over to the Coast Guard, which was the owner of the lighthouse compound at that time. Lightkeeper Gene Austin moved the building to Schoolhouse Road in 1972, though he and his wife, Shirley, didn't move in until 1990. Gene Austin was born in the Corolla Coast Guard Station, moved away as a child, then came back and served as caretaker of the Whalehead Club and as lightkeeper

Directions:
Look for the small, gray house on your left.

The Navy barracks, first located at the foot of the lighthouse, is now the home of Gene and Shirley Austin.

from 1964 until 1990. Shirley Austin has lived all but two years of her life within sight of the Currituck Beach Lighthouse, first in Waterlily across the sound, then in Corolla since 1959. Shirley recalls that when she moved to Corolla in 1959 with two children and one on the way, her family doubled the permanent population of the village.

24. <u>Gard House</u>

Not at all an original building of Corolla village, this charming old beach cottage was recently moved up the beach from Kill Devil Hills. It belonged to the Gard family from Elizabeth City and dates back to the 1930s. Rather than destroying this old house, as many people do today to make way for modern conveniences, the Gard family offered it to Doug and Sharon Twiddy, who have preserved some of the historic buildings of Corolla village. This was a much-loved house, and you can sense that even from the street. Inside the house there are three door jams that are full of names, dates and heights that represent many generations of growing children.

While the come-here house is an obvious outsider among the village architecture, its age

Directions:
Continue to the next house on your left.

Nellie Swain and Walter Austin around 1920.

and character could be seen as serving a purpose in the village today. An example of the Nags Head style of architecture, the house serves as a reminder of Corolla village's own distinct character. Look how vastly different things were constructed down the beach in days gone by. It gives us a sense of how Corollans developed a stylistic village all their own.

25. Boardwalk to Currituck Sound

The Currituck Sound played an important role in the early life of Corolla village. The village was always oriented more toward the calm sound than the unpredictable ocean, and it wasn't until vacationers arrived in the 1970s and '80s that the orientation of this area moved toward the beach.

In the older days, the Corollans' lives were intertwined with Currituck Sound. The sound supports a variety of fish, which were caught to eat. The fresh water and grasses of the sound attracted a multitude of waterfowl, which were hunted for food and to sell. The wealth of ducks also meant that the locals had jobs as guides for sportsmen who came to town. The villagers also went to and from the mainland across the sound to visit relatives. In the very early days of the village, a steamer ship would bring supplies that the villagers had ordered. Later, though, with the invention of cars, most Corollans drove up the beach to Virginia for supplies.

On the soundside were former public docks that served the village. One stretched far out to the deeper water of Currituck Sound. This was known as Lighthouse Wharf, or in later years, the Coast Guard Dock. It's great length allowed steamer and cargo boats from the mainland to approach the deep water at the end of the dock to unload supplies for the lighthouse. There was another dock called the Community Dock. Anyone who was traveling to or from the mainland embarked or disembarked at this dock. Just about everyone in the village had a boat of some sort, and small boats were left tied to this dock,

Photo Courtesy: Outer Banks Conservationists

Corolla postcard.

Directions:
Back at the corner of Schoolhouse Road and Corolla Village Road, turn left and walk back toward the Whalehead Club. Just after seeing the Keepers' House on the left, look for an opening in the trees and a CAMA sign on the right. Follow this narrow boardwalk to the sound.

A wide view of the area from the lighthouse to the Whalehead Club and south. The Community Dock and the Mailboat Dock are located on the sound in the bay located in the center of the picture. Notice the large number of structures on the beach. The largest building at the bottom is the Currituck Beach Lifesaving Station. Also notice how the beach goes almost to the lighthouse.

while larger boats had to be anchored off a ways in the sound. John Austin, who ran the local store in the mid-1900s, had a landing house down at the docks that supplied gas for these boats.

The Mailboat Dock was on the soundside as well. This was a shorter dock that the mailboat could pull up alongside. If the sound was frozen over or impassable due to weather, the village postmaster would have to drive on the beach to Virginia to get the mail. Corollan Norris Austin remembers one Christmas when his postmaster father had to drive to get the mail because the sound was frozen over for weeks and many of

the villagers had ordered their Christmas presents via mail from Sears and Roebuck. The mail quit coming by boat in the 1960s. 🐎

Directions:
Walk back across the lawn to the Whalehead Club.

Currituck Waterfowl Hunting & the Currituck Shooting Club

In the mid to late 1800s and early 1900s Currituck Sound's reputation was that of a "Sportsmen's Paradise." Canvasbacks, redheads, black ducks, mallards, widgeons, shovellers, teal, buffleheads, common ducks, snipe, blue peters, ruddy ducks, Canada geese, snow geese and tundra swan spent their winters on Currituck Sound, attracting great numbers of hunters and giving the local residents great opportunities. The Currituck Bankers practiced the occupation of "market hunting," killing waterfowl to sell on the market. Hunters would load their boats with ducks up to the hatches and take them across the sound to sell at Poplar Branch. The ducks were then shipped through Norfolk and on to dinner plates all along the East Coast.

It didn't take long for word about the incredible numbers of ducks on Currituck Sound to spread. In 1854, a New York businessman named Valentine Hicks hunted near Poplar Branch on the mainland and was astounded by the numbers of waterfowl he

John Williams, hunting guide, 1926.

saw. Hicks took this news back to his shooting pals in New York, and their trips south became more regular. By 1857, Hicks and a group of 14 other men had bought a sizeable chunk of land on the Currituck Banks. They built an eight-room clubhouse, and thus was established the Currituck Shooting Club. The club consisted

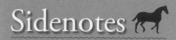

Sidenotes

Photo Courtesy: The Currituck Club

entirely of Northerners, who came for a couple of weeks each year. They spent all day in the marsh and on the sounds, and spent their nights indoors, dining, drinking and resting well.

During the Civil War, no one shot at the club, and, in fact, much of the club's boats, guns and ammunition was removed as the spoils of war and sold at the Currituck County Courthouse. In 1879, the Currituck Shooting Club members built a second clubhouse about 75 years away from the first. This second club still stands today, a testament to its solid construction. It is visible from the sixth green of The Currituck Club golf course.

The 1879 clubhouse was and still is grand. The first floor is a spacious clubroom, outfitted

A group of Northerners on the porch of the Currituck Shooting Club.

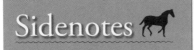

Sidenotes

for masculine group living. On the second floor are 21 individual bedrooms, enough to for each member to have a room of his own. There will never be more than 21 members at the club for this reason. The top floor is a large dormitory that was originally for guides.

After the Civil War, wealthy sportsmen flocked to the Banks, along with the waterfowl. Currituck Sound was widely known as the best waterfowl hunting region in the state. In the early 1900s, dozens of hunt clubs were established along Currituck Sound. As outsiders came to shoot, locals found additional work building boats, making ash push poles, carving decoys, building blinds, guiding, cleaning ducks, cooking and maintaining the clubhouses. Corolla Island (now the Whalehead Club) was one such club, finished in 1925.

Shooting, however, got a little out of control. There were so many waterfowl in the sound that some hunters became irresponsible. From 1888 to 1910, The Pine Island Club reported killing 72,124 waterfowl from 1888-1910, in other words, over 3,000 ducks a year. Stories of that same reckless killing abounded at the Currituck Shooting Club as well. In November 1885, two club members shot 423 waterfowl in one day. In November of 1887 seven members came back with 588 ducks.

As the numbers of ducks declined, laws were put into effect to prevent such massacres. In 1918, market hunting came to a halt with the passing of laws prohibiting the sale of waterfowl. Still, hunters could still shoot as many ducks as they wanted to and employ whatever tactics they wanted to get them, including baiting waterfowl and using live decoys. It wasn't until the 1930s that strict game laws were passed to shorten the season, lower bag limits and outlaw live decoys and certain types of guns. About that same time, an eelgrass blight lessened the population of ducks on the sound, requiring all the clubs to practice more waterfowl conservation.

Waterfowl hunting is still a great Currituck Sound tradition, though the numbers of ducks aren't anywhere near what they used to be. A few of the old clubs remain. The 146-year-old Currituck Shooting

Sidenotes

Photo Courtesy: The Currituck Club

Club is still in operation today, making it the oldest continuously operating private hunting club in the nation.

The old Currituck Shooting Club.

This view from the top of the lighthouse would have been much different 25 years ago.
All of the houses shown have been built since 1985.

Corolla Now

Getting There

Corolla is sequestered on the northernmost reaches of North Carolina's Outer Banks. Bordered on the east by the Atlantic Ocean and on the west by the Currituck Sound, with its northern border barred by a gate at the Virginia line, Corolla is a beach-lover's boondocks. Traveling here only amplifies its feeling of remoteness. You have three options in traveling here: arriving by water in a shallow-draft boat, landing on an airstrip in a small plane or motoring in via a long, curvy, two-lane highway.

Most travelers come to Corolla from the north, traveling down U.S. 64 then U.S. 158 from Virginia. At Kitty Hawk, North Carolina, U.S. 158 joins up with N.C. Highway 12 N., which leads directly to Corolla. The only problem is that every visitor to the northern Outer Banks – tens of thousands a week in the summer – has to travel this same two-lane highway in the same direction at the same time. Traffic can be a little trying on check-in, check-out and rainy days, but really it's nothing compared to a daily commute in the city. Some Corolla property and business owners are begging for the construction of a bridge that would lead from U.S. 158 across the Currituck Sound directly to Corolla, offering another way in and shaving as much as an hour off the trip. It might happen someday, but until then expect it to take twice as long as you'd think it would to travel 10 miles up N.C. Highway 12 in the summer.

Heading north from Kitty Hawk, N.C. Highway 12 winds through the small Dare County towns of Southern Shores and Duck before entering the realms of Currituck County, home of Corolla. Up until the development boom of the late 1980s, the Currituck Outer Banks was little-traveled and little-known, often referred to as North Carolina's last beach frontier. How things have changed today!

Don't let Corolla's out-of-the-way location fool you. This is no isolated outpost starved for vacation amenities. With shopping centers, restaurants, a major grocery store, a movie theater, a golf course, a world-class tennis facility, hotels, thousands of vacation homes and a whole range of services, Corolla is anything but desolate.

Sea Air Shuttle Service and Charter Flights

339 Audubon Drive (252) 453-3656

If you've ever driven onto the northern Outer Banks in the middle of the summer, you'll know what a valuable service this airline provides! Sea Air runs scheduled flights to and from Norfolk Friday through Sunday, Memorial Day to Labor Day, with a $150 one-way fare. Sea Air also provides year-round charter service to and from many destinations. Flying from D.C. can take as little as 50 minutes, and Richmond can be reached in 25 with Sea Air. Chartering a plane is ideal for day trips, business travel and special events. They have planes to accommodate from six to eight passengers and can occasionally match up passengers for a shared charter.

Sea Air also offers air excursions on the Outer Banks. These flights are a minimum of 30 minutes and can be customized to your sightseeing wishes. Imagine an aerial tour of lighthouses, shipwrecks and wild horses. The co-pilot will narrate the sights, and there are many opportunities for aerial photography. Sea Air is a fully licensed FAA commercial air carrier.

The Lay of the Land

The Currituck Outer Banks is a 20-mile stretch of sand on a 50-mile-long peninsula that reaches from the state of Virginia down to Oregon Inlet. There are no incorporated towns on Currituck

Services & Important Numbers

Corolla Library ..... (252) 453-0496

Corolla Chapel ..... (252) 453-4224

Outer Banks Chamber of
Commerce .... (252) 441-8144

Currituck County Sheriff's Office
.... (252) 453-2121

Currituck County Satellite Offices
.... (252) 453-8555

Tarheel Internal Medicine
(Walk-ins accepted)
.... (252) 453-8616

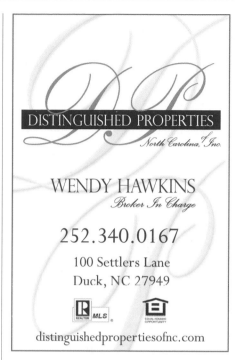

County's Outer Banks (nor are there any towns in the entire county, most of which is on the mainland). It is common nowadays for people to use the term "Corolla" to refer to the lower Currituck Outer Banks, though historically Corolla was only the name for the village near the lighthouse.

Upon entering Currituck County, you're greeted by mile after mile of immense homes packed together neatly along the oceanfront. Homes of astounding size and grandeur are the hallmark of Corolla, and weekly vacation home rentals, not hotel stays, are definitely the trend for tourists. The overwhelming majority of the houses on the Currituck Outer Banks were constructed within the last decade, most of them to accommodate vacation rentals. To stand out in this highly competitive market, Corolla homes must be fairly new, well-maintained and offer a surprising range of amenities, from oceanfront swimming pools to home gyms to professional-grade kitchens.

Back to Highway 12, in these parts known as Ocean Trail. Along your trip north, you'll notice the fancy signs for various planned community developments. The first you'll come to is Pine Island, site of opulent homes, a small airstrip, an incredible tennis center and, nearby, a new oceanfront Hampton Inn. Farther along N.C. Highway 12, you come to the massive development of Ocean Sands, where literally thousands of homes are spread out over several miles. On the west side of the road farther north is the Currituck Club, a golfing community with a prestigious links-style course, a clubhouse and restaurant, and exclusive homes. The Currituck Chamber of Commerce and the local ABC store are also located inside The Currituck Club.

Moving northward, you'll arrive at Corolla's only stoplight, marking the bustling intersection of commerce at

See **www.corollaguide.com** for full content, links & updates.

Ocean Trail and Albacore Street. Here you'll find Timbuck II, a grand shopping/dining/recreation complex; Monteray Plaza, with shops, restaurants, a major grocery store and the movie theater; plus stand-alone shops, gas stations, a bank and other services. Nearby are the developments of Buck Island, Whalehead and Monteray Shores. Farther north, you'll come to Corolla Light, another sprawling vacation development, this one with an abundance of amenities and family activities. Here you'll find the Inn at Corolla Light, the Corolla Light Sports Center as well as the Corolla Light Village Shops, with restaurants and stores.

The Whalehead Club and the Currituck Beach Lighthouse are situated in Currituck Heritage Park on the west side of the island north of Corolla Light. These are the two major tourist attractions in the area. Everyone loves climbing the lighthouse, and people return year after year to see the restoration work at the historic club. Soon there will be a new attraction at Currituck Heritage Park the Center for Wildlife Education, which is under construction at this time.

Just north of the lighthouse is old Corolla village, the site of this book's Walking Tour. Here you'll find old homes, quaint shops and friendly folk in an atmosphere that is very different from the rest of the beach. Beyond the park is a cluster of shops and a gas station, then another vacation development known as the Villages at Ocean Hill.

Just when you think you're getting somewhere, the paved road ends abruptly at the beach. You can keep going, however, driving on the beach into what the locals call the "four-wheel drive area," up to Pennys Hill, Swan Beach and Carova Beach, where there are a ton of

See **www.corollaguide.com** for full content, links & updates.

rental homes and a few full-time residents, including wild horses. About 10 miles up the beach, there's a gate blocking you from entering the state of Virginia. You have to turn back and go the way you came. 🐎

Corolla Culture

Corolla is predominantly a vacationland. The full-time, year-round population is only around 500, while the summer population can soar to more than 50,000 a week! It is estimated that there are nearly 5,000 rental homes on the 20-mile stretch of Currituck Outer Banks. The island is so narrow that there's only room for one main road N.C. Highway 12, a.k.a. Ocean Trail so you can imagine what summer traffic is like. Expect backups and delays upon arrival and departure and on rainy days in between. Everyone gets into their cars on rainy days, so if you're smart you'll do your shopping and attraction-hopping on sunny days.

The main tourist season in Corolla is, obviously, summer. The biggest crowds roll in and the rental prices go up from Memorial Day to Labor Day. Fall is heavenly on the Outer Banks because the crowds are thinner, the rates are a bit cheaper, all of the businesses are still open, the locals are in fabulous moods and the weather is still mild. And don't overlook winter and spring, when you can definitely get an accommodation bargain and some isolation, though not all of the businesses will be open. Businesses exist here to cater to the vacation population, so most every business owner takes a little break in the winter.

In Corolla you'll find all the amenities you want for a great vacation, but not a lot

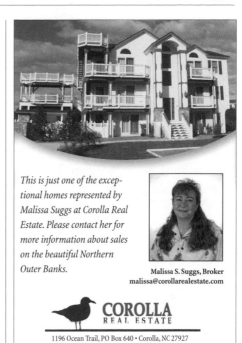

of the regular services you're used to back home. For those you may have to travel down the road to another Outer Banks town. For example, health care is offered in Corolla at a small center, but the closest hospital is in Nags Head, about 30 miles away.

No one really cares too much about the lack of super stores and necessities. Here, everyone's mind is on the beach. Corolla's beaches are clean and vast, with fine sand that gently slopes to the sea, and the water is warm. In the off-season you can find great isolated stretches of beach all to yourself.

Nightlife

If you're looking for nightlife, you'll find that Corolla's is somewhat subdued. Corolla has long been a sleepy village,

certainly not known as a happening spot for dancing until dawn, but recently more restaurants are adding live entertainment to the menu. Several places offer live music, among them are Guava Jelly's, Mike Dianna's Grill Room, and Dr. Unks bar in Tomato Patch Pizzeria. Sundogs Sports Bar is a great happening spot in the area with karaoke, games and live entertainment on weeknights (See our Restaurants chapter). If you want to plan some fun nights out, call around to a few restaurants to see what kind of entertainment they have lined up. If it's not lively enough for you, try to catch a band in the Nags Head area. Most Corolla residents and vacationers tend to prefer quiet nights a late dinner out, a stroll on the beach, maybe a movie. There's too much to do during the day to stay up all night.

While Corolla's draw isn't as a big recreation hotspot on the Outer Banks, it does offer kayak tours, Jet Ski rentals, surfing lessons, fishing charters, wild horse-finding trips, go-carts, a links-style golf course and tennis courts to keep you busy all day long.

Get Married in Corolla

Destination weddings are in. More and more brides and grooms are taking off to vacation locales, with friends and family in tow, to say their wedding vows. Corolla is an extremely popular spot for such events.

One thing couples are doing is renting a big oceanfront house, or several houses in a row, to house all their friends and family. Many couples hold their wedding

COROLLA CHAPEL

JOHN W. AUSTIN MEMORIAL
(INTER-DENOMINATIONAL)

Built in 1885
Re-dedicated in 1989
Pastor John O. Strauss

"No vacation to the Outer Banks is complete
without attending a service at the Corolla Chapel."
(comment made in a rental house guest book)

SCHEDULE OF SERVICES

IN SEASON	OFF SEASON
Memorial Day weekend through August 8:30 am 10:00 am	September through Sunday before Memorial Day Weekend 10:00 am

For unscheduled services call 252-453-4224

P.O. Box 64, Corolla, NC 27927
252-453-4224 • corollachapel@aol.com

Popular Wedding Destination

Portraits at the Beach

B r u c e   L o r e n z
photographer

since 1978

Historic Corolla Village
Corolla, North Carolina 27927

800.646.5812   www.blorenz.com

ceremony right on the beach, then throw a reception back at the house, either indoors or by the pool. Several of the vacation rental companies even have wedding planners on staff to assist couples with this type of event!

Other popular options include getting married on the grounds of the Whalehead Club or the Currituck Beach Lighthouse. Both of these sites rent out their incredibly inviting lawns for wedding ceremonies and receptions. At sunset, both locations are magical. Tents can be set up in case of rain. The Corolla Chapel in old Corolla village is a much-coveted wedding spot, and the Currituck Club has a marvelous space for receptions. And if you're looking for somewhere besides rental homes for your guests to stay, there are two large hotels, the Inn at Corolla Light and the Hampton Inn.

The Outer Banks is a hugely popular wedding destination, so you'll have no trouble finding high-quality service providers, as long as you reserve early. 🐎

Wedding Services

Wedding Accommodations

See the Accommodations section.

Wedding Cakes

Argyles Restaurant and Catering,
Debra Sinkage – (252) 261-7325

Beach Bread Company,
Carol Giese – (252) 261-5575

Cakes by Robin,
Robin Daniels – (252) 305-5365

Fishbones Sunset Grill,
Thom Seehafer – (252) 261-3901

See **www.corollaguide.com** for full content, links & updates.

Good Life Gourmet,
Steve and Susie Mace – (252) 480-2855

Great Cakes! of the Outer Banks,
Marsha Johnson – (252) 261-3403 or (252) 599-2235

Just Desserts,
Melinda Gregory – (252) 441-2931

Katering by Kim,
Kim Epps – (252) 441-7010

OBX Chefs2Go,
J. Wesley (Wes) Atkins – (252) 202-8851

Outer Banks Brewing Station,
Tina MacKenzie – (252) 449-2739

Sonny's Creative Kitchens & Provisioning Co.,
Sonny Williams – (252) 491-9969

Tasteful Creations Cakes,
Norlina Kelly – (252) 449-9162

Tullios Pastry Shop, Bakery and Café,
Tom and Dawn Amoruso – (252) 261-7111

Wedding Caterers

1587 Restaurant and Catering,
Anne Pond – (252) 473-1404 Ext. 119

Argyles Restaurant and Catering,
Debra Sinkage – (252) 261-7325

Bay Club Catering,
Sosie Hublitz – (252) 453-6653

Beach Bread Company,
Carol Giese – (252) 261-5575

Black Pelican Catering,
Jason Smith – (252) 261-3171

Bluewater Culinary Services,
Rob Mitchell – (252) 449-2433

Carolina Catering Company,
Bo and Emma Perkins – (252) 207-1643

Chip's Wine and Beer Market,
Chip Sellarole and Tammy Kennon – (252) 449-8229

Culinary Magick,
Gwen Hart, Brian Marti – (252) 202-8888

Firehouse Wine Cellar & Brew,
Ermino Mazzarino – (877) 771-WINE (9463)

Good Life Gourmet,
Steve and Susie Mace – (252) 480-2855

High Cotton NC BBQ,
Will & Sherry Thorp – (252) 255-2275

Jolly Roger Restaurant,
Carol Ann Angelos – (252) 441-6530

Katering by Kim,
Kim Epps – (252) 441-7010

Kelly's Outer Banks Restaurant and Tavern,
Mary Ann Newman – (252) 441-4116

The Kitchen Witch Catering,
Mary M. Thrasher – (252) 453-2260

Lone Cedar Catering,
Ron Kneasel – (252) 441-5405

Mako Mikes,
Bill Martin – (252) 480-1919

Mike Dianna's Grill Room,
Mike and Lindsey Dianna – (252) 453-4336

OBX Chefs2Go, J.
Wesley (Wes) Atkins – (252) 202-8851

Outer Banks Brewing Station,
Tina MacKenzie – (252) 449-2739

Outer Banks Original Chocolate Fountain Co.,
Kevin Wescott – (252) 202-8436

Penguin Isle,
Tom Sloate – (252) 441-2637

Pigmans Bar-B-Que,
Bill Ulmer – (800) 442-5207

See **www.corollaguide.com** for full content, links & updates.

Queen Anne's Revenge,
Wayne and Nancy Gray – (252) 473-5365

Red Sky Cafe,
Chef Wes Stepp – (252) 261-8646

Seamark Foods,
Ginger Farrow – (252) 261-2220

Sonny's Creative Kitchens & Provisioning Co.,
Sonny Williams – (252) 491-9969

Sooey's BBQ and Rib Shack,
Beaman L. Hines, Sr. – (252) 441-2798

Waterfront Trellis,
Linda Rogers – (252) 473-1723

Weeping Radish Brewery & Bavarian
Restaurant, Uli Bennewitz – (252) 473-1991

Windmill Point Restaurant,
Scott Ramm – (252) 441-1535

Wedding Photographers

A Photo Moment,
Jeanic Cubin – (757) 235-3316

Aircastles,
Larry Swain – (252) 453-0078

Ascension Photography,
Gordon Kreplin – (252) 449-8997

Axford Hand-Painted Black and White
Photography, Mary Claire Axford –
(252) 480-2593

Basnight Photography,
Mary Basnight – (252) 473-3933

Beach Productions,
Julie Dreelin – (252) 207-2293

Brooke Mayo Photography,
Brooke Mayo – (252) 599-0720

Chris Bickford – (252) 202-2399

Custom Photography Limited,
Marian and Michael Linett – (252) 480-6431 or
(757) 498-0205

Daryl Law Photography,
Daryl Law – (252) 480-6332

Deborah Sawyer Photography,
Deborah Sawyer – (252) 473-4800

Donna Holcomb, Photographer,
Donna Holcomb – (252) 453-0765

Eye Candy Digital Video,
Mike Martine – (252) 435-2763

F2 Photographic Design,
Mollie Isaacs – (800) 645-9958

Island Photography,
Mike and Allie Hawkins – (252) 489-8003

J. Aaron Trotman Photography,
Jim and Laura Trotman – (252) 480-1070 or
(877) SMILES8

Jeff Greenough Photographer,
Jeff Greenough – (866) 204-3451

Kristi Midgette Photography
– (252) 573-8229

Lisa Arnold Photography,
Lisa Bernard-Arnold –(866) 267-8711

Lorenz Fine Photography,
Bruce Lorenz – (800) 646-5812

Photography by Geri,
Geri Shipman – (252) 473-3351

Seaside Photography,
Lisa A. Griggs – (252) 305-4747

Shelley Chamberlin Photography,
Shelley Chamberlin – (252) 453-4366

Shooters at the Beach,
Biff Jennings – (252) 480-2395

See **www.corollaguide.com** for full content, links & updates.

Simona Photography,
Simona Price – (252) 207-2431

Thomas Gartman Photographer,
Thomas Gartman – (866) 275-6679

Walter V. Gresham III Photography,
Walter V. Gresham III – (800) 887-1415

Wedding Disc Jockeys

A Music Man for all Seasons,
John Harper – (252) 473-4528

DJ Steve the Dream,
Steve Allen Thomas – (252) 261-4709

Hot Music Mix,
Don Wornstaff – (800) 546-7625

KDH Sound and Light,
Doug Leal – (252) 480-2844

Metro Rental,
Rob Waddington – (866) 490-3535

Music By Tommy,
Tommy Midgett – (252) 473-6848

Outer Banks DJ,
Michael Stoffel – (252) 441-1076

Soundwavz Entertainment,
Don J. Vaquera – (252) 261-6583 or (866)
OBX-WAVZ

Wedding Equipment

Metro Rental -- (252) 480-3535

Ocean Atlantic Rentals,
Joe Southern – (252) 261-4346

Outer Banks Computers & Music (sound
system rental), Mark or Rich – (252) 441-3002

Wedding Musicians

1 Man Band/Keyboardist,
Buzz Bessette – (252) 202-1029

A Classically Trained Pianist/Singer,
Angela Furr – (252) 473-9177

Angelo Music,
Angelo Sonnesso – (866) 269-1380

Coyote,
Marcy Brenner and Lou Castro – (252) 256-2081

Greg Shelton – (252) 207-1648

Kim Kalman –(888) 826-9822

Outer Banks Chamber Players,
Jane Brown – (252) 480-2493

Perfect Occasions Wedding Music,
Janice Gross – (252) 453-3670

Roy Murray Music Studio,
Roy Murray – (252) 480-1532

Scott Franson – (252) 449-8355

Showstoppers of the OBX,
Diane Russ – (252) 480-9556

Sue Dean Violinist/Heart Strings & Ivory,
Sue Dean – (252) 473-6686 or (252) 267-2112

The Crowd,
Rick Ostlund – (252) 207-1070

The Touch,
Scott Guthrie – (252) 453-9365

The Wedding Flute,
Tanya Holland – (252) 453-6824

The Wilder Brothers,
Kevin Roughton – (252) 491-9986

Salon, Spa and Beauty Services

Arbonne International,
Marsha Riibner-Cady – (800) 967-6627

Barefoot Bridal Massage,
Ali Berryman – (252) 202-3277

Better Body Massage and Spa,
Lori Hillyer – (252) 305-1176

Diva's Day Spa & Salon,
Stephanie Mikos – (252) 255 1772

Eden Day Spa and Salons,
Mary C. DiDario – (252) 255-0711

Hair Designers,
Stacy Sheetz – (252) 480-4247

Hairicanes Salon,
Veelee Donahue – (252) 261-7889

Luxury,
Katrina Migliore – (252) 449-2474

Mary Kay Independent Consultant,
Patricia Quinn – (252) 473-9969

The Sanderling Resort & Spa,
Belinda Anderson – (252) 449-6664 Ext. 517

The Spa at Corolla,
Nancy Lenthall – (252) 453-9799

Waterfront Salon and Spa,
Connie Bateman – (252) 473-5323

Wedding and Reception Sites

108 Budleigh,
Bonnie Hudgins – (252) 473-2208

1587 Restaurant and Catering,
Anne Pond – (252) 473-1404 Ext. 119

A & A Atlantic Outer Banks Cruises,
Stuart Wescott – (252) 473-1475

Ann's Wedding Bells,
Ann Bell – (252) 473-2635

Bay Club Catering at Shallowbag Bay,
Sosie Hublitz – (252) 473-6255

Bordeaux Events,
Marie Castro –(888) 8BORDEAUX

Burrus House Inn and Waterfront Suites
– (252) 475-1636

Cameron House Inn,
Julie Thompson – (800) 279-8178

Cape Hatteras KOA Campground,
Mo Vandesteene – (800) 562-5268

Comfort Inn Oceanfront South,
Samantha J. Atkins –(800) 334-3302

The Currituck Club,
Eric Kallestad – (252) 453-9400

Downeast Rover,
Mark Kopp – (252) 473-4866, (866) SAIL-OBX

The Elizabethan Gardens,
Tama Creef – (252) 473-3234

Fishbones Sunset Grill,
Thom Seehafer – (252) 261-3901

Hampton Inn & Suites Outer Banks, Jennifer
Leidecker – 800-HAMPTON

The Island Guest House – (252) 473-2434

Kinnakeet Shores Recreation Association,
Kelly Gibbs – (252) 995-3302

Mallards Marsh,
Deborah Sawyer – (252) 473-4883

Nags Head Golf Links, The Players Grill,
Richard Beetle – (252) 441-8073

North Carolina Aquarium on Roanoke Island,
Michele Bunce – (866) 332-3475

See **www.corollaguide.com** for full content, links & updates.

Penguin Isle,
Tom Sloate – (252) 441-2637

The Saltaire,
Ron Forlano – (252) 255-5409

The Sanderling Resort & Spa,
Nicole Fontana – (800) 701-4111

Tale of the Whale,
Dan Bibey – (252) 441-7332

The Village Beach Club,
Ina Phelps – (252) 480-2222

The Waterfront Trellis,
Linda Rogers – (252) 473-1723

The Weeping Radish Brewery & Bavarian
Restaurant,
Uli Bennewitz – (252) 473-1991

The Whalehead Club,
Tammy Keller – (252) 453-9040

White Doe Inn,
Kristi Midgette – (888) 280-4819

Windmill Point Restaurant,
Scott Ramm – (252) 441-1535

Wedding Planners and Coordinators

Joan's, Keeland Owens – (252) 453-8844

Aaponi Designs,
Beth Markham – (252) 473-4883

Affairs to Remember,
Laura Tillett – (252) 216-9122

Ann's Wedding Bells,
Ann Bell – (252) 473-2635

Anne's Seaside Simplicity,
Anne Pond – (252) 473-4993

Avery Little Detail,
Avery Harrison – (252) 441-1880

Bella Vita,
Barbara Miller – (252) 573-8247

Black Tie Affair,
Emma Wilson Perkins – (252) 449-4889

Bordeaux Events,
Marie Castro – (252) 441-8183 or (888)
8BORDEAUX

Carolina Wedding Company,
Rev. Shirley Ann Gross – (252) 449-2453

House of Celebrations,
Beth Pallett – (888) 280-4819

Ocracoke Occassions,
Nancy Leach – (252) 928-3401

Proper Setting,
Nannette Jernigan – (252) 441-8166

Sugar Snap Events,
Shirley Cook –(866) 480-9990

The John Gillam Company Ltd.,
John Bond Gillam III – (252) 441-7752

Wedding Florists

BLOOMS Design Studio,
Renee Landry – (252) 255-0798

Brooks at Vista Florist,
Brooks – (888) 449-4080

Holiday House Weddings,
Kim Stetson – (252) 473-6938

Island Bouquets and Baskets by Nicki,
Anita Baker – (252) 449-4787

Joan's,
Keeland Owens – (252) 453-8844

Nags Head Florist – (252) 441-1330

Ocean Wreath,
Betty Laughridge – (252) 480-2080

Sea Breeze Florist & Gifts,
Tori or Brandi Ferebee – (252) 261-4274 or (800) 435-5881

Seamark Florist,
Robbie Harrell – (252) 441-4121

Jewelers

Cara Magnus Celtic, Ltd.,
Joan Young – (252) 261-8110

Dare Jewelers,
Nancy – (252) 441-1112

Diamonds 'n Dunes,
Ken Kelley and Eileen Alexanian – (252) 473-1002

Jewelry by Gail,
Judy Lyon – (252) 441-5387 or (800) 272-9817

Lady Maye,
Heather Maye Sakers – (252) 599-6814

Lone Wolff Trading Company,
Chris Wolff – (252) 449-5111

Low Tide Jewelry,
Margaret Miller – (252) 441-2644

Natural Creations Jewelers,
Tim Crank – (252) 255-2015

Silver Bonsai Gallery,
Ben and Kathryn Stewart – (252) 475-1413

Wedding Officiant

Ann's Wedding Bells,
Ann Bell – (252) 473-2635

Black Tie Affair,
Rev. Del Wilson, Jr. – (252) 449-4TUX

Carolina Wedding Company,
Rev. Shirley Ann Gross – (252) 449-2453

Leslie Buck/Saints Alive! Ministries,
Rev. Leslie Buck-Ferguson – (252) 987-1469

Outer Banks Wedding Ceremony,
Rev. Tanya K. Young – (252) 473-1818 or (252) 423-0099

Susan W. Bryant, Chaplain – (252) 232-3420

Weddings Outer Banks,
Rev. Eugene McLawhorn – (252) 491-9287 or (252) 202-3113

Your OBX Wedding,
Rev. Jay Bowman – (252) 216-6676

Chapels

Corolla Chapel
John O. Strauss – (252) 453-4224

Roanoke Island Garden Wedding Chapel,
Ann Bell – (252) 473-2635

Limos and Transportation

Coastal Carriage,
George Garrick – (252) 491-8201

Grouper's Limousine Service,
Kevin Wescott – (252) 202-8436

Island Limousine,
Keith Stone – (800) 828-5466

Karat Limo,
Nick and Elner Meekins – (252) 473-9827

Sandy Beach Tours,
Sandra Morrison – (252) 441-9800

The Beach Bus,
Lyndi Bascue – (252) 255-0550

See **www.corollaguide.com** for full content, links & updates.

Corolla Attractions 🐎

The main attraction on Corolla is the miles of beaches lined with fabulous vacation rental homes. You'll find plenty of other things to do here including lots of shops and restaurants.

The Whalehead Club and the Currituck Beach Lighthouse are the two major tourist attractions in the area. Everyone loves climbing the lighthouse, and people return year after year to see the restoration work at the historic club. A new attraction opening soon at Currituck Heritage Park is the Center for Wildlife Education.

Just north of the lighthouse is old Corolla village. Here you'll find old homes, quaint shops and friendly folk in an atmosphere that is very different from the rest of the beach.

Just when you think you're getting somewhere, the paved road ends abruptly at the beach. You can keep going, however, driving on the beach into what the locals call the "four-wheel drive area," up to Pennys Hill, Swan Beach and Carova Beach, where there are a ton of rental homes and a few full-time residents, including wild horses. About 10 miles up the beach, there's a gate blocking you from entering the state of Virginia. You have to turn back and go the way you came.

The Whalehead Club

Currituck Heritage Park,
N.C. 12, Corolla   **(252) 453-9040**

The Whalehead Club is a historic house museum on the northern Outer Banks. The grand residence, dressed in bold yellow and striking copper, stands on a vast green lawn bordering the Currituck Sound. At first sight of the 23,000-square-foot Art Nouveau home, so out of place in the Outer Banks landscape, it's immediately apparent that it has an intriguing past and a fascinating story to tell.

The Whalehead Club, on the National Register of Historic Places, sat empty and abandoned for nearly 25 years until Currituck County bought the building with the intent of restoring it. Since 1999, the county has painstakingly restored the house to exactly the way it looked when it was completed in 1925 (then known as Corolla Island). Any architectural changes that were made by owners other than the Knights have been removed.

The near $5 million restoration began

with the replacement of the copper roof. The exterior of the house and boathouse are exactly the same paint colors as the originals, as are the interior walls. The interior has been completely restored, from the coffered ceilings down to the $120,000 cork floors. Many of the original fixtures and details remain: The water lily motif carvings again stand out near the dining room ceiling, the duck head door handles are back in place, the Tiffany glass light fixtures shine again, the mahogany trim and woodwork has been refinished.

A team of researchers has tracked down as much information as possible to make the restoration as accurate as possible. Recently, the research team has been focusing its efforts on finding as much of the original furnishings as possible. Mrs. Knight's piano and Mr. Knight's iron safe and portrait were some of the only original furnishings left in the house when the restoration began. China and a few pieces of furniture, including a Louis Majorelle tea table, have been returned. The dining room is completely furnished as it was originally, including Tiffany sconces and water lily shades. An exhibition on display in the basement showcases some of the Knights' and other owners' treasured artifacts, as well as a prized collection of antique decoys.

The copious research has also turned up much information about the original owners Edward and Marie Louise LeBel Knight themselves. Local lore had always portrayed Mrs. Knight as a sharp shooting ruffian who was indignant about being ostracized from Outer Banks hunt club society. But as the researchers uncover information about Mrs. Knight, this seems unlikely. We now know that Mrs. Knight was educated, wealthy and socially accepted in Newport society. In her city clothes and ways, she was very different from the women of the Currituck Outer Banks and likely shocked the locals. This led to misperceptions about her, which have been passed down through the years. The staff at the Whalehead Club now has every reason to believe she was a dignified, well-respected woman.

The Whalehead Club staff gives guided tours of the house interior. The tours offer a wealth of information about the architectural style of the house, the first owners, the history of Corolla and the northern Outer Banks, and the transforming restoration of the home. Guided tours are the only way to see the house,

Photo Courtesy: Whalehead Preservation Trust

Artifacts from the Corolla Island and Whalehead Club eras and local waterfowl heritage can be found in the basement.

but you wouldn't want to see it without the guide anyway. The guides are locals who are knowledgeable about the area and its history.

The tour begins with a video. The guide then takes the group throughout the living areas, the private rooms, the servants' quarters and the 6,000-square-foot basement. In the basement are finely crafted exhibits that further detail the information learned on the tour. The exhibits focus on the history of the area, the Currituck Sound and its waterfowl hunting culture, the original and subsequent owners and the restoration of the clubhouse.

The Museum Shop stocks tasteful Whalehead Club souvenirs such as picture frames and ornaments made from the original copper roof plus books, postcards and memorabilia.

The Whalehead Club is open from April through Thanksgiving with special holiday hours in December. Tours of the house are offered daily starting at 10 a.m. The last tour is at 5 p.m., though after daylight savings the last tour is at 4:15 p.m. Cost is $6 for adults and free for children ages 8 and younger. You can also schedule a Behind the Scenes Tour; they run daily at 11 a.m. and 4 p.m. Behind the Scenes Tours are by reservation only and are appropriate for ages 13 and older.

Several specialty tours debuted in 2005, proved immensely popular, and will be offered again for the 2006 season. They include a Ghost Tour, which is given at 5 p.m. daily and costs $5 per person. A Children's Tour and Ghost Hunt is offered daily at 10 a.m., costs $5, and is appropriate for ages 6-12. Special pricing is available when you combine a house and specialty tour.

The grounds of the Whalehead Club are perfect for a relaxing afternoon outdoors away from the beach. The grounds are also available for rent for weddings and receptions. Other special events scheduled at the Whalehead Club in the summer of 2006 include: Wildlife Education with the N.C. Wildlife Resources Commission, Memorial Day through Labor Day, Monday through Friday, 10 a.m. and 2 p.m.; Wild Horse Days, June 16, 4 p.m. to 8 p.m.; Whalehead Club Arts Festival entitled, "Under the Oaks," June 21 and 22; the July Fourth Festival and Fireworks on Monday, July 4, 6 p.m. to 11 p.m.; and the Summer Concert Series on the Lawn, 7 p.m. every Thursday in July with the NC School of the Arts and in August with Outer Banks artists.

Outer Banks Center for Wildlife Education

Currituck Heritage Park, N.C.
Highway 12, Corolla   (252) 453-0221

Wildlife Education programs are held in Currituck Heritage Park Monday through Friday. Programs include sound habitat exploration, decoy carving and fishing in the sound. Most programs are free. Call to register in advance. The North Carolina Wildlife Resources Commission's exciting new Outer Banks Center for Wildlife Education is expected to open in 2006. The 22,000-square-foot building will house an auditorium with a video program, an exhibit hall, classrooms and a gift shop. Exhibits will focus on conservation, waterfowl and hunting heritage, natural history, local heritage, ecology and fishing. Highlights of the exhibits will be an aquarium and real-life marsh exhibit. The location of the center

The stately and historic Corolla Lighthouse can be seen from many vantage points throughout the village and is surrounded by beautiful grounds.

is on the sound between the Whalehead Club and Currituck Beach Lighthouse. See our Recreation chapter.

Currituck Beach Lighthouse

Currituck Heritage Park, N.C.

Highway 12, Corolla   (252) 453-4939

The red-brick Currituck Beach Lighthouse towers above the northern Outer Banks landscape at the village of Corolla. Visitors can climb the winding staircase 214 steps in all to the top of the lighthouse for a panoramic view of Currituck Sound, the Atlantic Ocean and the Currituck Outer Banks. Inside the lighthouse, at the base and on the first two landings, there are museum-quality lighthouse exhibits. On the way up or down, stop to learn about the history of coastal lighthouses, the Fresnel lens and the Currituck Beach keepers.

The 162-foot lighthouse was first lit on December 1, 1875. Onsite keepers, who lived in the surrounding buildings, operated the lighthouse until it was automated in 1939. With automation, the lighthouse no longer required a regular keeper. The lighthouse and its outbuildings fell into disrepair for 40 years until a nonprofit group called Outer Banks Conservationists (OBC) stepped in to save the lighthouse in the 1980s. OBC renovated the keepers' buildings to re-create their past glories and restored the lighthouse to make it safe to climb. In July 2003, The U.S. Department of the Interior awarded OBC ownership of the lighthouse.

See **www.corollaguide.com** for full content, links & updates.

It costs only $6 to climb the lighthouse, and children 7 and younger climb for free. The lighthouse is open daily from mid-March through November. Climbing hours are 10 a.m. to 6 p.m., except in November, when they close at 5 p.m. Climbers must go up 15 minutes before closing. During extreme weather, the lighthouse is closed to climbing.

The main building, the Double Keepers' House, is not open to the public. You can go inside the small Keeper's House, which was transformed into the Museum Shop and stocks everything lighthouse-related you could ever imagine. T-shirts, hats, books, postcards, blankets, taffy, ornaments, jewelry, magnets, figurines and more fill this former keeper's residence.

CAMA Sound Boardwalk

Currituck Heritage Park

This boardwalk cuts through a small portion of swamp forest and brackish marsh. The variety of flora and fauna you'll see here is astounding. Sweet gum, red maples, black willows, live oaks and loblolly pines are intertwined with wild muscadine grapes, Virginia creeper and winged sumac. Shrubs like American holly, wax myrtles, yaupon and bayberry fill in the lowlands, while plants like swamp mallows, morning glory, ferns, honeysuckle, pennywort add texture and color to the landscape.

Toward the sound, tall reeds and cat-tails swish in the breeze. The boardwalk ends at a nice resting spot on Currituck Sound, an absolutely perfect place to watch the sunset. Animals you might see along the way include nutria, deer, raccoons, muskrats, red or gray fox, river otters, possums, turtles, snakes and a great variety of birds, including songbirds, wading birds, osprey, terns, killdeer, gulls and others, depending on the time of year.

Wild Horses Exhibit at the Corolla School

Corolla Village Road and Schoolhouse Road
(252) 457-1185

In the summer of 2004, the schoolhouse launched an educational exhibit on the Corolla wild horses. It is fun for the entire family with interactive, hands-on activities, photography and historical information. Call for details about special activities on holidays.

Village Garden

Corolla Village behind the Lighthouse Garden shop

Be sure to make a stop here when you're out shopping in Corolla Village. The public is invited to tour the garden anytime.

The 4,000-square-foot garden, funded by Twiddy and Co. Real Estate, features five raised beds, an herb garden, a butterfly garden, a garlic and basil garden, vegetable garden and a cutting garden. A "found" garden is being developed with all native species. The garden is planted and maintained by Amy Stewart, who puts her efforts into heirloom and older varieties of plants. Many of the seeds grown here are those that would have been available at the turn of the last century, from 1900 to 1920.

When you drop by, you'll likely find Amy or one of her assistants at work. Ask them questions about the unusual plants you'll see in the garden. In the summer you may find a painter at work here too. The garden is interesting year round.

See **www.corollaguide.com** for full content, links & updates.

Currituck Banks National Estuarine Research Reserve Access Trail

Soundside, End of N.C. 12, north of Corolla

This beautiful boardwalk leads two-thirds of a mile from the road to the sound, traversing through maritime evergreen forest, swamp forest and brackish marsh. Along the way, you'll see live oaks and loblolly pines, yaupon, holly, bayberry and wax myrtle, plus, closer to the water, sedges, cattails, black needlerush and giant cordgrass. You may see signs of animals, like scat or tracks, or possibly the animals themselves. Birders love this boardwalk because it gives them the ability to go deep into several habitats without getting so mucky.

Along the boardwalk are a couple of places to rest and an information kiosk. At the end, the boardwalk has bench seats that look out over a creek and the sound. It's serene, quiet and absolutely beautiful on the soundside.

Part of the 960-acre North Carolina National Estuarine Research Reserve, this area is protected in its natural state for use as a natural laboratory. Much of the land in this area is protected. The U.S. Fish and Wildlife Service manages the 4,000-acre Currituck Banks National Wildlife Refuge north of here for waterfowl, wading birds and shorebirds.

Corolla Surfing Museum

Corolla Surf Shop   **Monteray Plaza**
(252) 453-WAVE (9283)
Timbuck II Shopping Village   (252) 453-9273

Housed in all locations of Corolla Surf Shop, the Corolla Surfing Museum is a collection of classic surfboards that were acquired by Steve and Brant Wise. The boards, hanging from the ceilings of the shops, represent many of the small, experimental designs of the 1960s. There are boards by Dewey Weber, CON, Surfboards Australia, Bing, Gordon and Smith, Bunger, Hobie and others, with a good representation of collectible boards from both the East and West coasts.

You'll also see memorabilia and photography. Many surfers are impressed with the CON Ugly and are awed by the 1930s wooden hollow board and the reproduction of the solid-wood 80-pound surfboard. If you want to learn more about the roots of surfing, don't miss seeing these collections. 🐎

Sidenotes 🐎

Corolla Wild Horses

If you go to the northern reaches of the Currituck Outer Banks, beyond the paved road and into the wilder realms, you'll likely encounter

Photo Credit: M. Parker

Corolla horses resting in the morning sun.

some of the free-roaming Corolla wild horses. These exotic equines have roamed the rugged northernmost Outer Banks for more than four centuries, and geneticists have proven that they are descendants of 16th-century Barb horses, Spanish and Portuguese stock that was bred on the Barbary Coast of North Africa.

It is not known exactly when and how the horses got to the Outer Banks, but the widely held belief is that they came ashore with early European explorers. Both Spanish and English explorers traveled with Barb horses and other livestock, and both groups explored this area in the 16th century. Either the explorers brought the

See **www.corollaguide.com** for full content, links & updates.

If you go to the northern reaches of the Currituck Outer Banks, beyond the paved road and into the wilder realms, you'll likely encounter some of the free-roaming Corolla wild horses. These exotic equines have roamed the rugged northernmost Outer Banks for more than four centuries, and geneticists have proven that they are descendants of 16th-century Barb horses, Spanish and Portuguese stock that was bred on the Barbary Coast of North Africa.

It is not known exactly when and how the horses got to the Outer Banks, but the widely held belief is that they came ashore with early European explorers. Both Spanish and English explorers traveled with Barb horses and other livestock, and both groups explored this area in the 16th century. Either the explorers brought

Sidenotes

After 14 horses were killed by automobiles the herd was fenced to remain north of the paved road. The fence runs ocean to sound and leaves the horses to roam freely and safely on 15,000 acres.

Photo Credit: Lloyd Childers

the horses here and left them behind or else the horses swam ashore in shipwrecks. Though the

Sidenotes

If you go to the northern reaches of the Currituck Outer Banks, beyond the paved road and into the wilder realms, you'll likely

Until the last few years horses roamed wild through Corolla village.

encounter some of the free-roaming Corolla wild horses. These exotic equines have roamed the rugged northernmost Outer Banks for more than four centuries, and geneticists have proven that they are descendants of 16th-century Barb horses, Spanish and Portuguese stock that was bred on the Barbary Coast of North Africa.

It is not known exactly when and how the horses got to the Outer Banks, but the widely held belief is that they came ashore with early European explorers. Both Spanish and English explorers traveled with Barb horses and other livestock, and both groups explored this area in the 16th century. Either the explorers brought the horses here and left them behind or else the horses swam ashore in shipwrecks. Though the Corolla wild horses have clear Spanish origins, their isolation on the Outer Banks for more

COROLLA RECREATION

Looking for something to do beyond the beach at Corolla? You won't have trouble finding fun here. From a wild-horse search to a kayak tour, from go-carts to 18 holes on the links, there are plenty of recreational opportunities available on the northern Outer Banks.

Nightlife

If you're looking for nightlife, you'll find that Corolla's is somewhat subdued. The area has long been a sleepy village, certainly not known as a happening spot for dancing until dawn, but recently more restaurants are adding live entertainment to the menu. Several places offer live music, among them Guava Jelly's, Mike Dianna's Grill Room and Dr. Unks bar in Tomato Patch Pizzeria. Sundogs Sports Bar is a great happening spot in the area with karaoke, games and live entertainment on weeknights (See our Restaurants section.) If you want to plan some fun nights out, call around to a few restaurants to see what kind of entertainment they have lined up. If it's not lively enough for you, try to catch a band in the Nags Head or Kill Devil Hills area.

Most Corolla residents and vacationers tend to prefer quiet nights, a late dinner out, a stroll on the beach, maybe a movie. There's too much to do during the day to stay up all night.

Bicycle Rentals

Corolla Jeep Rentals and Tours

Whalehead Bay Shoppes,
N.C. Highway 12   (252) 453-0077

Corolla Jeep Rentals and Tours has both beach cruisers and mountain bikes for rent by the day or the week. They can deliver the bikes to you.

Ocean Atlantic Rentals

Corolla Light Town Center,
N.C. Highway 12   (252) 453-2440

When visiting Corolla, you'll need your car from time to time to get to the grocery store or between shopping centers. Otherwise, ditch the car and pedal everywhere you go. Ocean Atlantic Rentals rents single-speed beach cruisers that are perfect for lazy cruising. They will deliver the bikes to you.

Just for the Beach Rentals

Ocean Club Centre   Monteray Plaza
(252) 453-9388,   (252) 453-6106

Make like a local and pedal around Corolla on a beach cruiser. Just for the Beach Rentals will deliver the bikes to you.

Boating

If you have your own boat and need to get it in the water when you are in Corolla, there's a public boat ramp at the Whalehead Club that allows access to Currituck Sound.

Outer Banks Charter Fishing Adventures/Corolla Bait and Tackle

Corolla Light Town Center, N.C. Highway 12 and Austin Street, Timbuck II Shopping Village
(252) 453-9500, 453-9690

Corolla Bait and Tackle offers a pontoon-boat trip to the winery at Knotts Island. You take a short boat trip across the sound, participate in a wine tasting at the beautiful vineyards, then motor back to Corolla. They also offer two-hour sunset cruises where you take a relaxing cruise around the sound, see Monkey Island, birds and other wildlife. Be sure to bring binoculars, snacks and drinks. Want a little more action? Ask about the full range of fishing trips offered here; for more information see our Fishing section.

Climbing

Carolina Outdoors

Monteray Plaza,
N.C. Highway 12   (252) 453-3685

The Outer Banks is extremely flat, but if you're looking to get vertical, check out the climbing wall at Carolina Outdoors. The 26-foot climbing wall is located in the Monteray Plaza courtyard. You get two climbs for $7, and no reservations are necessary.

Fishing

Corolla Bait and Tackle

Corolla Light Town Center, N.C. Highway 12
and Austin Street, Timbuck II Shopping Village
(252) 453-9500

Keith Cummings, owner of Corolla Bait and Tackle, goes beyond the call of duty when it comes to sharing his fishing knowledge. Everyone who comes through the door gets fishing instruction. This full-service tackle shop sells every major brand of tackle for fresh and salt water, plus gear, fresh bait, crabbing supplies, ice and more. The advice is free. Corolla Bait and Tackle rents rods, reels and crab pots. Surf-fishing classes are offered as well. See Outer Banks Charter Fishing Adventures, below, for guided fishing opportunities.

Local fisherman Billy McOwen is all smiles after landing this huge Striper in the surf in Corolla.

Corolla Jeep Rentals and Tours

Whalehead Bay Shoppes
(252) 453-6899, (252) 453-0077

Corolla Jeep Rentals and Tours offers a variety of fishing charters, held in either the sound or the ocean, for a half, three-quarter or full day. Depending upon which trip you choose, you can catch mackerel, marlin, tuna and dolphin. The boats carry up to six passengers, and if you don't have a group of six ready to go, they can accommodate you with a make-up charter. All fishing tackle is included, so all you need to bring is lunch.

Outer Banks Charter Fishing Adventures/Corolla Bait & Tackle

Corolla Light Town Center, N.C. Highway 12
and Austin Street, Timbuck II Shopping Village
(252) 453-9500, (252) 453-9690

With all kinds of trips to choose from, Corolla Bait and Tackle can arrange a fishing trip that's perfect for you — just tell them what kind of fish you're after. For a family outing, try the two-hour Introduction to Fishing trip, held on a pontoon boat in the Currituck Sound. It's fun for anyone of any age who wants to learn about fishing. They also offer inshore, offshore and backcountry fishing trips, even big game safari fishing trips. You can choose from half-, three-quarter and full-day trips. They can also accommodate make-up trips, which means they can help you join an offshore charter if you don't already have a six-person party to go with you. See our Boating section for more about trips to the Knotts Island winery.

Tideline Charters

(252) 261-1458, (252) 473-3906

Captains Clay Hauser and Jay Bender run inshore and intermediate fishing

---

See **www.corollaguide.com** for full content, links & updates.

Photo Credit: Outer Banks Visitors Bureau

Last winter some of the largest Striper blitzes we've seen in a decade occurred in the surf just north of Corolla.

charters from the Currituck Sound to the Albemarle Sound and the ocean waters. Sound charters are in 17- to 20-foot Carolina-built skiffs that can launch at the Whalehead Club's public boat ramp or in Kitty Hawk Bay. Ocean charters out of Oregon Inlet are on board a 34-foot boat that docks in Pirates Cove Marina. All fishing equipment is included. Captain Clay recommends booking a charter to fish for striped bass, or rockfish as it's called locally, anytime from Thanksgiving to Valentine's Day. He thinks the best striped bass fishing on the East Coast is out of Oregon Inlet and says that it's not uncommon to catch stripers up to 35 pounds. You can even do a little whale-watching while you're out.

TW's Tackle Shop

Monteray Plaza,
N.C. Highway 12　　　　　(252) 453-3339

TW's is a well-respected Outer Banks tackle shop, with locations in Nags Head and Kitty Hawk as well. The Corolla location sells all the fishing gear, sportswear and bait you'll need for the whole family to enjoy fishing in the sound

or ocean. TW's has a large selection of lures, jigs, bottom rigs, nets, crabbing supplies and more. They stock fresh bait like shrimp and mullet and lots of frozen baits. You can rent rods and reels here. Best of all, the folks at TW's offer lots of free advice for everyone from the novice fisherman to the experienced angler. See our Shopping page for more about the sportswear and home décor items sold here.

Go-Carts

Corolla Raceway

Timbuck II Shopping Village,
N.C. Highway 12　　　　　(252) 453-9100

The Corolla Raceway features one large track with 16 super-fast Indy cars. For the tamer ones in your crowd, there are freestanding, gas-powered bumper cars. The onsite arcade is a hit with the kids. The Raceway is open Easter through November, and from Memorial to Labor Day they have a snack bar stocked with treats.

See **www.corollaguide.com** for full content, links & updates.

Views of the sound and ocean are breathtaking from many holes at the Currituck Club.

Golf

The Currituck Club

N.C. Highway 12

(252) 453-9400, (888) 453-9400

The Currituck Club is a 6,888-yard, par 72 golf course situated on 600 acres of pristine wetlands along the Currituck Sound. The links-style course, designed by Rees Jones, has received widespread accolades from the golfing press, including a top 25 ranking in North Carolina by Golf Digest. The designer took great care to leave as many natural elements as possible around the course, which is set amid dunes, wetlands and marsh. Views of the sound and ocean are breathtaking from many holes, and wildlife sightings are common. Call well in advance for a tee time at this renowned course. To improve your game, The Currituck Club also offers a full driving range, lessons and golf clinics. The clubhouse has a restaurant, bar and lounge, a pro shop, locker rooms, bag storage and a private members' lounge.

Hiking Trail

Audubon Wildlife Sanctuary Pine Island

An unmarked trail leads through this 5,000-acre wildlife sanctuary, a protected habitat for birds, deer, rabbits and a variety of plants. Park at The Sanderling Inn to access this 2.5-mile soundside path through a portion of the sanctuary.

Running

OBX Marathon, Gateway Bank Half-marathon & Kelly's Hospitality Group Fun Run

For information and to register, go to:

www.obxmarathon.org

On Sunday, November 12, 2006, you can participate in the first ever OBX Marathon, presented by the Outer Banks Visitors Bureau, The Gateway Bank Half-

See **www.corollaguide.com** for full content, links & updates.

marathon or the Kelly's Hospitality Group Fun Run. The marathon begins in Kitty Hawk, travels on through Kill Devil Hills and around the Wright Memorial, goes through Nags Head and ends on Roanoke Island. The Gateway Bank Half-marathon begins by Jockey's Ridge in Nags Head and ends on Roanoke Island. Walkers are welcome, so there's no excuse not to be involved. There is a $25,000 prize purse for the OBX Marathon. The OBX Marathon is the official 2006 U.S. Track and Field North Carolina Association Marathon Championship.

Miniature Golf

The Grass Course

N.C. Highway 12   (252) 453-4198
    The Grass Course offers 18 holes of miniature golf on all-natural grass. Holes are par 3s, 4s or 5s, and all ages can play here. There's a deli and snack shop on site. The course is open all day, until 10 or 11 p.m. on summer nights. It's next to the Corolla Light Sports Center.

Lighthouse Mini-Golf

N.C. Highway 12   (252) 453-3452
    Next to the Corolla Post Office and Winks Texaco, Lighthouse Mini-Golf is a great place for family entertainment. Kids love to play 18 holes of putt-putt here.

Movies

RC Theaters Corolla Movies 4

Monteray Plaza,
N.C. Highway 12   (252) 453-2999
    For first-run major movies, this is the

only place to be on the northern beaches. The Corolla movies are open seasonally, from May through Labor Day and then again from Thanksgiving through New Year's Day. Movies are shown seven days a week. Call the hotline for movie information or check a local newspaper, like The Coastland Times or The Outer Banks Sentinel. On rainy summer days they run extra showings in the mid-morning or early afternoon.

Here are some tips for off-roading

• Do not attempt to drive on the beach unless you have a four-wheel-drive vehicle.
• Let the tires' air pressure down to between 20 and 25 psi.
• Try to stay in the ruts that were made by cars traveling before you.
• Stay off the dunes and away from wildlife.
• All laws that apply to the roads apply to beach. Drivers must be licensed, safe and sober, and vehicles must be legal. The maximum speed limit is 35 m.p.h., or 15 m.p.h. when within 300 feet of beachgoers, swimmers or anglers.
• If you do get irreparably stuck in the sand, call A-1 Towing at (252) 453-4002.
• ATVs can be used only by Currituck County property owners, and the operators must get a permit from the Currituck County Satellite Office, (252) 453-8555. Non-property owners are not allowed to operate ATVs in this area.

Off-Roading

N.C. Highway 12 ends abruptly just past Corolla Village, but that doesn't mean you have to stop there. Beyond the highway there are 10 more miles of beach.

The easiest way to explore this area is to take a guided four-wheel-drive tour (see the Wild Horses and 4WD Nature Tours section below). If you'd rather explore the area on your own, vehicles are allowed to drive on the beach year round. It is lawful to drive north/south on the beach. The property on the west side behind the dunes is private, and non-property owners should stay out of that area.

Segway Tours

Back Country Outfitters and Guides

Corolla Light Town Center,
N.C. Highway 12
(252) 453-0877

The Segway looks like so much fun that when you see people gliding around Corolla on them, you'll want to try one too! The Segway is a self-

balancing, two-wheeled electric vehicle built for one. You stand on a small platform to ride, and the Segway responds to your movements. Simply shifting your weight forward makes it go, standing straight up puts the brakes on, and leaning back makes you go backward. Turning the handle controls your turns.

At Back Country Outfitters and Guides, they'll take you through a short certification course, which usually lasts 30 to 40 minutes, though they say it only takes a few minutes to get comfortable on the Seg. After you're acclimated, Back Country offers a gliding tour of Historic Corolla Village. The tour lasts about one to one and a half hours, and you'll view historic landmarks and learn about the village. If you're looking for an adventure, you'll want to try the Spanish Mustang Reserve tour. The off-road tour begins

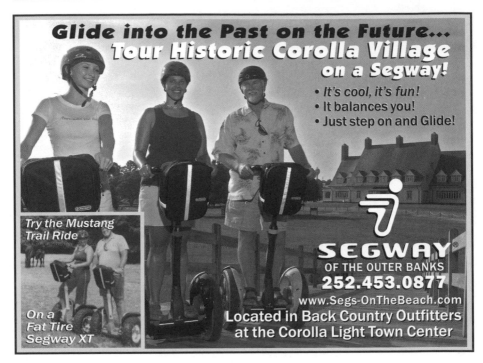

with a four-wheel drive on the beach up to a Maritime forest, where you'll ride the off-road version of the Segway through Back Country's private Spanish Mustang Reserve. The off-road tours last about three hours and reservations are necessary.

Skateboarding

Island Revolution Skatepark

Corolla Light Town Center,
NC Highway 12   (252) 453-9484

Island Revolution Skatepark was brand-new in 2005. It is over 5,000 feet of extreme fun for the skateboarder in the family, and everyone else will enjoy observing. The skatepark is concrete and is built with diverse features like two bowls, a quarter pipe, street course, grind bars and vertical drop-ins. Safety equipment

must be worn at all times. A CPR-certified attendant oversees the park. Bikes and scooters are not allowed. Boards and pads can be rented at Ocean Atlantic Rentals. Passes can be purchased at Island Revolution Surf Shop.

Surfing

Corolla Surf Shop

Monteray Plaza   Timbuck II Shopping Village
(252) 453-WAVE and 453-9273

If you don't know how to surf or want to get better at it, take a lesson through the surf school at Corolla Surf Shop. The two-hour introductory group lessons cover all the basics and include board and wetsuit rental, all for just $60. As long as the waves are good and you're in pretty good shape, the instructors can almost guarantee

See **www.corollaguide.com** for full content, links & updates.

Gary Smith, owner of Corolla Surf Shop in a competion.

they'll have you standing up by the end of the lesson. Intermediate and advanced classes are also offered, as are private lessons. The minimum age to participate is 9 years old. All instructors are CPR trained, and most are trained as lifeguards too. Lessons are offered daily in the summer and by request in the off-season. Contact them ahead of time to sign up if you're visiting during the busy summer months. You can call the shop or sign up on their website. Corolla Surf Shop also rents surfboards, wetsuits, bodyboards and skimboards.

Island Revolution Surf Shop

Corolla Light Town Center   (252) 453-9484

Catch a surf lesson here while you're in town. Experienced surfers teach the lessons, which include a surfboard rental and wetsuit if needed. Choose from a group, couples or private lesson. The group lesson is kept small, at three to four people. Lessons last two hours. The minimum age for lessons is 10. Don't forget to bring along beach essentials, such as sun block, beach towels and a drink.

Just for the Beach Rentals

Ocean Club Centre   Monteray Plaza
(252) 453-9388, (252) 453-6106

Just for the Beach Rentals rents surfboards known as soft-tops, which are ideal for beginning surfers. Surfboard rentals are $15 a day or $45 a week. They also have body and skim boards for rent for $8 a day or $20 a week. Just for the Beach can deliver the boards to you.

Ocean Atlantic Rentals

Corolla Light Town Center   (252) 453-2440

Ocean Atlantic Rentals has all the equipment you need for surfing, body boarding or skim boarding. They even have swim fins, which are great for body boarding. If the water is chilly when you're here, they rent wetsuits to keep you warm while you tackle the waves. Ocean Atlantic Rentals delivers.

Spas

Eden Day Spa

Monteray Plaza   (252) 453-0712

Eden Day Spa and Salon offers a variety of luxurious treatments to relax and pamper you. Spa services include body polishes and wraps, European facials, nail care and body treatments in their vichy shower and a hydrotherapy tub. Choose from Swedish, deep tissue or aromatherapy massage. They have six treatment rooms and the salon, which offers all hair services plus makeup application and facial waxing. Eden is an Aveda concept salon. They feature a full line of Aveda's quality products, which use natural ingredients. Call to schedule an appointment.

Spa at Corolla

510 Old Stoney Road in Ocean Club Centre
midway between Duck and Corolla
(252) 453-9799

Slip on a robe and nestle down into a comfy chair in the relaxation room to reflect, to think, to leave the world at the door. Experience peace even before starting your treatments! This upscale spa offers much more than a massage and a pedicure. The spa services here are ritualistic experiences that allow you the time and space to focus on your own wellbeing. From custom facials to signature body polishes, hydrotherapy or shirodhara, you'll relax your body, soothe your mind and refresh your spirit. In the busy summer season appointments book well in advance, so plan ahead by visiting their website or calling the spa before you leave home.

Tennis and Fitness

Pine Island Racquet & Fitness Club

N.C. Highway 12 between Corolla and Duck
(252) 453-8525

Who says you have to miss a workout while on vacation? This club sports a fitness and health center complete with cardio and circuit training equipment. They offer elliptical trainers, Cybex machines, free weights, treadmills and rowing machines. The club is open to the public, so you can pay to work out for a day or get a membership for a week or longer.

For tennis players, the Pine Island Racquet Club is a still a tennis lover's dream. Choose from play on three indoor Plexi-cushion hard courts, heated or air-conditioned depending on the weather,

or two outdoor clay courts. Lessons and
clinics for children and adults are available
from P.T.R. pro Rick Ostlund and staff.
Reservations are suggested for court times,
and play costs $28 per court. The club is
open every day but Christmas Day. In-season
hours are from 7 a.m. to 7 p.m. Off-season
hours are from 8 a.m. to 8 p.m. Monday
– Friday and 8 a.m. to 5 p.m. on weekends.
The pro shop sells racquets, clothes and
tennis accessories and provides stringing
services. Want to set up a match? The club
has a player referral list to organize matches.

Just for the Beach Rentals

Ocean Club Centre   Monteray Plaza
(252) 453-9388, (252) 453-6106
Didn't realize there would be so many
great tennis courts in Corolla? If you
didn't pack your racket, you can rent one at
Just for the Beach Rentals.

WaterSports

Carolina Outdoors

Monteray Plaza   (252) 453-3685
Carolina Outdoors has ocean kayaks
(the sit-on-top style) available for rent.
They offer single and tandem kayaks. No
reservations are necessary.

Corolla Watersports Rentals and Tours

Inn at Corolla Light,
N.C. Highway 12   (252) 453-6141
The Inn at Corolla Light has a 400-
foot pier on the Currituck Sound that's
a great launching place for several water
sports. You can rent a Jet Ski to zoom
around on the water or even take a Jet Ski
tour. If you're not into speed, rent a kayak
for some quiet paddling. If you'd like to
do some crabbing but don't have the right
equipment, you can rent a net and bucket
here and drop your bait from the pier.

Corolla Kayak Company at Corolla Jeep Rentals and Tours

Whalehead Bay Shoppes   (252) 453-0077
Corolla Kayak offers guided tours
through a section of marsh near the old
Currituck Inlet Hunt Club. Paddlers are
shuttled up to the four-wheel-drive area
where the tour begins. The area covered
by this three-hour tour is completely
surrounded by a U.S. Fish and Wildlife
Refuge and goes through marsh creeks
and along the sound shores. You'll often
glimpse wild horses. Corolla Kayak also
offers a two-hour tour through Whalehead
Bay. You'll leave from the shop and paddle
around where birds and other wildlife are

See **www.corollaguide.com** for full content, links & updates.

plentiful. This tour can be led by a guide or self-guided. All tours are by reservations; call for times and prices. Corolla Kayak also offers ocean kayak rentals, and they can deliver them to you.

Just for the Beach Rentals

Ocean Club Centre   **Monteray Plaza**
         (252) 453-9388, (252) 453-6106
     Want to plan your own kayak tour? Just for the Beach Rentals has kayaks available for rent, the sit-on-top style, for single, double or triple paddlers. They deliver; call for details.

Kayak Corolla

Back Country Outfitters and Guides
Corolla Light Village Shops,
N.C. Highway 12 and Austin Street
                              (252) 453-0877
     One of Kayak Corolla's most popular tours is the 4WD and Kayak Expedition. The start of this three-hour-plus adventure is the Wild Horse Safari (see Wild Horse Tours) in which you board a comfortable Suburban and take off for the northernmost beaches. The driving tour culminates with wild horse sightings near Carova. There, your kayaks await you. After a brief refresher on paddling, you're off into the Currituck Sound for an hour-long-plus guided paddle in a private wildlife reserve where there are no other people. Heaven! Reservations are a must; call for times and prices.

Kitty Hawk Kayaks & Watersports

Timbuck II Shopping Village,
N.C. Highway 12   (252) 453-6900
     On the sound at the backside of Timbuck II, Kitty Hawk Watersports rents Waverunners, party boats, sit-on-top and sit-in kayaks, sailboats, windsurfers, two- and four-seat pedal boats, body boards and surfboards. Guided kayak ecotours are offered in the morning and afternoon and at sunset. Parasailing is also offered here. Kitty Hawk Watersports has a retail store in Timbuck II, but that is not where you book the tours or rent gear. Go to the sound and look for the water sports building and pier on the sound.

Kitty Hawk Kites

Timbuck II and Stan White Building,
N.C. Highway 12
          (252) 453-8845, (877) FLY THIS
     Kitty Hawk Kites offers guided kayak ecotours beginning at the pier at the Inn at Corolla Light. You can book the tours at either of the Corolla store locations or by calling the toll-free number. Make reservations for the tours, as they are usually booked solid in season. You can also rent kayaks from Kitty Hawk Kites.

Ocean Atlantic Rentals

Corolla Light Town Center,
N.C. Highway 12   (252) 453-2440
     If you want to rent kayaks to do some exploring on your own, Ocean Atlantic Rentals will bring them to you. You can rent kayaks for exploring the sound or riding the ocean waves.

See **www.corollaguide.com** for full content, links & updates.

Come take a two-hour tour of the north beaches in one of our air-conditioned suburbans. Our knowledgeable guides will take you on an off-road adventure to see the wild ponies. Along the way, you will enjoy stories of a bygone era, local lore and ecology.

Age 12 and under Half-Price!
Ask about our Package Deals!

$5 Off
Wild Horse Tours

Located at the Inn at Corolla Light
252-453-8602

Wild Horse & 4WD Nature Tours

There was a time when you could look out your rental cottage window and see a wild horse nosing around in your trash can or eating your grass, but, for the good of the horses, that is no longer so. The wild horses were relocated to the four-wheel-drive area north of Corolla, so you must have an off-road vehicle if you want to see them.

The easiest way to see the horses is to take a guided tour with an outfitter. The guides know exactly where to look for the horses, they know how to drive in the sand and they know a lot about the history of the area, making for a much more enlightening trip on your part.

If you do see the horses, keep at a respectful distance of at least 500 feet away. Look but do not touch or feed these wild animals. Bring binoculars with you and you'll get an up-close look without disturbing the horses. (See the Corolla wild horses section below.)

Beach Jeeps of Corolla

Corolla Light Town Center   (252) 453-6141

Beach Jeeps of Corolla is a great way to see the northern beaches of Corolla and the area's famous wild horses. The Jeep Safari is a self-guided tour that follows a preplanned GPS route. You'll see wild Spanish ponies, Penny's Hill, Swan Beach, and the canals of Carova Beach. On North Swan Beach you'll see the Wash Woods Lifesaving Station. In addition to the wild ponies, you may see deer, red fox and dolphins. Tours last two-and-a-half hours and are a great way to explore the secluded northern beaches and see local wildlife in their natural habitat.

Bob's Off Road Wild Horse Adventure Tours

Inn at Corolla Light, N.C. Highway 12
(252) 453-8602

Bob's tours last two hours and incorporate quite a bit of local history to complement the sightseeing. At the beginning, your guide will take you past the Whalehead Club and lighthouse and through Corolla Village, showering you with some interesting lore. Then it's up to the four-wheel-drive area, where you'll see the horses grazing in their natural habitat. Bob's tours are given in air-conditioned Suburbans and can accommodate up to seven people. Call for details and reservations. All tours have a money back guarantee.

See **www.corollaguide.com** for full content, links & updates.

Whalehead Bay Shoppes

(252) 453-6899, (252) 441-8875
Corolla Jeep Rentals and Tours offers guided tours of the off-road area, including their own private 400-acre Hunt Club. Guided tours are two hours long and conducted in comfy 15 passenger vans or Suburbans. You can also rent a soft-top Jeep and take off on a self-guided tour, with the aid of the navigation systems provided in the Jeeps. These tours last two-and-a-half hours and the navigation system sends you on a course where wild horses are usually spotted. You'll see beautiful, remote beaches and wildlife.

Corolla Outback Adventures

N.C. Highway 12   (252) 453-4484
Corolla Outback Adventures, run by Corolla native Jay Bender, is a two-hour, 20-mile guided tour of the northern Outer Banks. On this trip you tour via four-wheel all-terrain vehicles. Corolla Outback Adventures owns more than 200 acres on the northern beaches, about a third of which is a reserve partnership with the Corolla Wild Horse Fund. This private reserve area allows people on the tour to see the horses grazing in their natural habitat. On the way to the reserve, the guide stops to talk about the history and ecology of the area. Tours are offered every two hours in the summer, and Corolla Outback is open from April to December.

Wild Horse Safari

Back Country Outfitters and Guides
Corolla Light Town Center,
N.C. Highway 12   (252) 453-0877
Scott Trabue's Wild Horse Safari is a 30-mile round-trip tour to Carova Beach, where horses are always sighted. The guided tour takes place in a comfortable Suburban that can seat up to eight people. During the two–and-a-half-hour tour, the naturalist guide will tell you about the history, nature and ecology of the northern Outer Banks, and you'll see wildlife, a petrified forest, a giant sand dune, a life-saving station and hear the tale of a buried village. You'll travel beaches, dunes and a maritime forest. This tour company has exclusive access to the Spanish Mustang Reserve where the tour stops for photos and to hear about the mustang's heritage. Reservations are required.

Wildlife Programs

Outer Banks Center for Wildlife Education,
Currituck Heritage Park   (252) 453-0221
Corolla's Wildlife Resources staff offers great Wildlife Education programs all summer long. Most programs are free and teach participants about such topics as birding, sound ecology, ocean ecology, animal tracking, orienteering, sea turtles, fishing, decoy carving and much more. Programs are held Monday through Friday, are about an hour long and are open to all ages. Most programs begin at the picnic shelter. Check local newspapers and attractions listings for a schedule, or call the program coordinator at the number above to inquire. They can arrange for group programs and also offer teacher workshops. It's best to sign up for the programs ahead of time to ensure you get a space. 🐎

Island Revolution

SKATE PARK

Corolla's Surf & Skate Headquarters

island revolution

252-453-9484

Located at the Corolla Light Town Center

COROLLA LIGHT
— TOWN CENTER —

Everything You Want Is Here!

New building with 14 new shops and eateries!

Adventure Tours

Arcade

Bagels

Bakery

Bait & Tackle

Bar & Seafood Grill

Beach Rentals

Bike Rentals

Books & Music

Breakfast

Cappuccino

Catch & Release Fish Pond

Children's Clothing

Convenience Store

Deli

Fudge

Gelateria

Ice Cream

Italian Restaurant

Jeep & Jetski Rentals

Kayak Rentals

Men's & Women's Clothing

Nascar & Collegiate Clothing

Pizza & Subs

Playground

Real Estate Rentals & Sales

Seafood Market

Skate Boards

Skate Park

Souvenirs

Sportswear

State Fishing License

Steak & Cheese

Surf Boards

Surfing Lessons

T-Shirts

*Shopping & dining
beautifully located
with views of the
Currituck Beach Lighthouse*

COROLLA SHOPPING

orolla is all about retail recreation. Shopping opportunities are abundant in and around the three major shopping complexes — Timbuck II, Monteray Plaza and Corolla Light Town Center — and in the old Corolla village area.

Almost all of the shops here are locally owned and operated, so they each have an individual character and offer things you won't see at home. You could easily spend a whole day shopping in Corolla when you need a little break from the beach. Just remember that on rainy days, everyone else will want to be shopping with you. Vacationers are notorious for getting in their cars on rainy days and heading straight to the malls.

If you've got family members in tow, don't worry, because most of the shopping centers here offer diversions other than shopping. Timbuck II Shopping Village has plenty of recreational opportunities, like water sports and go-carts, to keep the family entertained while you shop. At Monteray Shores Shopping Plaza, there's a climbing wall and movie theater. Corolla Light Town Center features a brand-new skatepark that's as much fun for curious onlookers as it is for skaters.

Ocean Club Centre at the Currituck Club

Corolla ABC Store

Ocean Club Centre   **(252) 453-9628**

In North Carolina, all liquor and spirits other than beer and wine are sold at special package stores by the name of ABC Stores. The Corolla location is at 500 Hunt Club Drive. It's near the south entrance of the Currituck Club, a golfing community off N.C. Highway 12. Checks are not accepted. Beer and wine are sold at grocery and convenience stores.

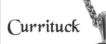

Old Stoney's Beer and Wine

501 Old Stoney Road,
Pine Island area   (252) 457-1050

Old Stoney's specializes in adult beverages, including imported, domestic and microbrew beers, and wine of all kinds. They also stock grocery items here, like milk, bread and eggs. Old Stoney's carries some beach necessities like sunscreen, soft drinks, ice, coolers and chairs. Need cash? They have an ATM.

Just for the Beach Rentals

501 Hunt Club Drive, Pine Island area
          (252) 453-9388

If you couldn't bring it or forgot it, don't worry. Just for the Beach probably has it, and they can deliver it to you before you even miss it. Here you can rent baby equipment like cribs and strollers, cottage equipment like grills, recreational equipment like bikes, kayaks and surfboards and beach equipment like umbrellas and chairs. Just for the Beach is also a retail shop with a bunch of beach souvenirs, toys and gift items.

Bluewater Seafood Market

Hunt Club Drive,
Pine Island area   (252) 453-9921

Bluewater Seafood offers fresh-caught fish, clams, crabmeat, scallops, lobsters and other treats from the sea. They also carry everything else you need to prepare a delicious seafood dinner at home, including fresh produce, marinades, spices and seafood tools. Or call ahead and have your crabs, shrimp, lobster and crab legs steamed to order. For a real seafood feast, order one of their steamer buckets to go; just select your favorite seafood to fill it. Stop here on the way out of town to take local seafood home to your freezer. Bluewater is open every day in season.

Timbuck II Shopping Village

Corner of Ocean Trail and Albacore Street
          (252) 453-4343

Timbuck II, named after its developers, Tim and Buck Thorton, is a shopping, dining and entertainment village with more than 60 shops and restaurants. The shopping, dining and entertainment venues span the range of interests, and the whole family could truly spend a day here. Restrooms are around every corner, and there's a playground in the center.

See **www.corollaguide.com** for full content, links & updates.

Brew Thru

Timbuck II Shopping Village (252) 453-2878

The original drive-through beverage store has been on the Outer Banks for more than 25 years. The Corolla location offers ice-cold beer, wine, soft drinks, gas and the world-famous Brew Thru T-shirts.

Carolina Moon

Timbuck II Shopping Village (252) 453-9046

This is one of the quintessential Outer Banks gift shops, with locations in Corolla, Duck and Kill Devil Hills. The Corolla store specializes in jewelry and likely has the best selection of earrings on the Outer Banks. You'll find eclectic, one-of-a-kind pieces of jewelry, including estate pieces, as well as unique cards and clothes the likes of which you won't find anywhere else.

Casual Creations

Timbuck II Shopping Village (252) 453-9775

This women's boutique offers everything you need for the vacation lifestyle, including casual wear and lots of fun accessories. You'll also find golf accessories, unique purses, one-of-a kind outfits and much more.

Corolla Bait and Tackle

Timbuck II Shopping Village (252) 453-9690

This tackle shop carries all the basic fishing necessities like rods, reels, fresh and frozen bait, even crabbing supplies. The shopkeepers have a wealth of knowledge and love to share tips on fishing their local waters. They also rent equipment, run charter fishing excursions and host surf fishing classes.

Corolla Book, Card and Gift Gallery

Timbuck II Shopping Village (252) 453-4444

This huge store will occupy several members of the family for quite a while. The book section offers best sellers plus great local and regional titles. Then you've got the gift section with an array of postcards and greeting cards, T-shirts, games, candy, shell lamps, candles, fragrances, figurines, mugs, prints, Beanie Babies and stuffed animals and toys, and that's not nearly the half of it. You can also find the popular D. Morgan prints here.

Corolla Candles

Timbuck II Shopping Village (252) 457-0233

This candle shop isn't like the others. If you'd like to literally take some of the beauty of the beach home with you, check

this place out. Local candle artists Chuck and Janet Sowers make a line of beautifully colored candles that are embedded with shells picked right from Outer Banks beaches every morning. The shop also carries candles from more than 50 of America's finest candle makers. You'll also find a full line of Burt's Bees natural skin care products as well as incense, Windstone Sculptures and other local art.

Corolla Surf Shop

Timbuck II Shopping Village (252) 453-9273

Gary Smith, the affable owner of Corolla Surf Shop, is the father of surfing culture on the northern beaches. With lessons, rentals, sales and repairs, Gary strives to introduce surfing to everyone who wants to learn and to keep the local surfers happy. He sells more than 100 new and used boards, by both local shapers and nationally known names. At all three locations you can arrange for surf lessons (students must be at least 9 years old) and rent surf equipment. The surf shop also sells a great variety of surfwear, sunglasses, sandals and accessories for the whole family. (See the write up on the Corolla Surf Museum in Attractions.)

Corolla Surf Shop

Timbuck II Shopping Village (252) 453-9280

This new location, the second in Timbuck II, for Corolla Surf Shop opened in the spring of 2006. Like all the other locations, you can arrange for surf lessons here (for 9 and older) and rent surf equipment. This location also has great surfwear styles for the entire family plus a large selection of high performance sunglasses and sandals. But what's unique for this store is its collection of surf memorabilia – artwork, CDs and more – that can help you express your surfing lifestyle. They're located next to Groupers.

Corolla Wine, Cigar, Gourmet

Timbuck II Shopping Village (252) 453-6019

Previously North Banks Wine Shop, Corolla Wine, Cigar, Gourmet has moved into a new soundview location in Timbuck II. They carry a large selection of wines from all over the world and continue to take a special interest in local wines and feature regional vineyards. The walk-in humidor is stocked with premium cigars. You'll also find a huge selection of specialty beers, champagne, gourmet foods and a host of wine paraphernalia like stemware, wine tools, even wine-scented candles. Sunset wine tastings with a sound view are held every Wednesday, and walk-in wine tastings are available daily.

The Cotton Gin

Timbuck II Shopping Village (252) 453-4446

For the feeling of an old-time country market, step into The Cotton Gin in the big, red barn-like building at the entrance to Timbuck II. Headquartered on mainland Currituck County, The Cotton Gin has been a coastal shopping tradition for nearly 40 years. You'll find seasonal and souvenir apparel including decorative and holiday sweaters, home accessories, collectibles, Teddy bears, waterfowl carvings, books, cards, prints, even fine wine from the local Sanctuary Vineyards.

Dog Nutz

Timbuck II Shopping Village (252) 453-9955

Does a pooch rule your roost? Do you go gaga over every dog you see? Dog Nutz

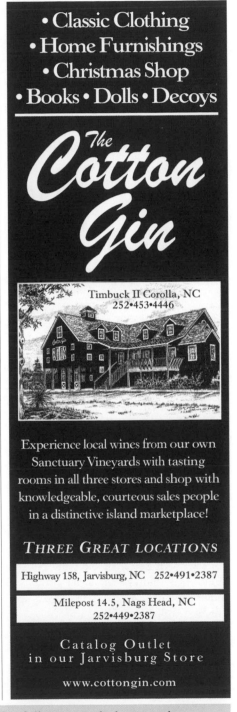
See **www.corollaguide.com** for full content, links & updates.

corolla
wine
g a
gourmet

Large selection
of Fine Wine
including local NC & VA wines

Plus...
Walk-in Humidor
& Premium Cigars

Specialty Beer & Champagne
Gourmet Foods
Fine Ports
Gift Ideas

www.nbxwine.com
Weekly Wine Tastings
call for details
252.453.6048

New Soundview Location
in TimBuck II, Corolla

The Fudgery

Timbuck II Shopping Village (252) 453-8882

Don't you hate it when people say
that chocolate fudge is sinful? Sometimes
it's just a necessity. The Fudgery's creamy
concoctions can satisfy any sweet tooth.
Your mind will be boggled at the variety
of flavors from dark chocolate to peanut
butter to rocky road, even New Orleans
praline. The fudge is all theatrically
prepared right before your eyes on marble
slabs and served by the thick slice. Check
out their chiller fudge – it's the perfect way
to enjoy the treat on a hot summer day.
You choose the ice cream then the fudge
or other sweets to add to it, and they mix it
up right in front of you.

get the picture?/The Cottage

Timbuck II Shopping Village (252) 453-2922

For all your vacation-photo needs, get
to get the picture? One-hour photo is the
top draw here, but you'll also find cameras,
batteries and film. The Cottage gift shop
has unique frames, local photography,
T-shirts and home accents designed to
make summer memories last all year. Here
you can also find a local photographer
who specializes in casual group portraits
– perfect for preserving memories of
family get-togethers.

is the store for you. Here, everything is for
the canine crowd, from doggie beach gear
and toys to everyday supplies and breed-
specific gifts. There are a few things for cat
and horse people too.

Dolphin Watch Gallery

Timbuck II Shopping Village (252) 453-2592

This is an eclectic gallery with a
soothing atmosphere, perfect for calming
overloaded senses after a day of shopping.
This gallery features original fine art from
pottery, jewelry, carvings and etchings to
stained glass, mosaics and metal works.
Inquire about the custom stained-glass and
mosaics work done by local artists. Look
for the popular Danish-designed jewelry
by Pandora. They have beautiful, original
watercolor and oil paintings, and custom
framing is available. Dolphin Watch Gallery
is open year round..

The Glass Shop

Timbuck II Shopping Village (252) 453-3999

Renee Hilimire uses glass as the
backdrop for her stunning painted designs.
Several design collections are available
on stemware, place settings and serving
pieces. The pieces are amazing alone but
make more of an impact when collected
as part of a set or mixed and matched

See **www.corollaguide.com** for full content, links & updates.

with other designs. If you're afraid your glassware won't make it home, The Glass Shop will ship it for you.

Good Vibes Video

Timbuck II Shopping Village (252) 453-3503

Next to the gas station south of the main shopping village, Good Vibes offers video and DVD rentals and sales and video game rentals. You can also rent DVD players, VCRs and Playstation 2 game systems. This summer they'll have coffee available to sip while you peruse the selection.

Gourmet Kitchen Emporium and Confectionary

Timbuck II Shopping Village (252) 453-4227

This shop is sure to please not just cooks but also those of us who love to eat! In addition to tabletop ware and kitchen supplies, they carry North Carolina gourmet products and other specialty foods, candies, coffee beans and tea. They also offer gift baskets — just order in advance and you can create your own or have them customize one for you with goodies from the shop.

Gray's Department Store

Timbuck II Shopping Village
                    (252) 457-1058, 453-4994

It seems that everywhere you look on the Outer Banks there's a Gray's Department Store, and here are two more in Timbuck II. This is one of most popular stores on the beach for good reason. Gray's offers the largest selection of Tommy Bahama and Fresh Produce sportswear on the Outer Banks. Plus you'll find souvenir T-shirts, sweatshirts and hats alongside sportswear for the whole family. This smaller store has the largest variety of kids clothing but also carries adult sportswear.

Hair-i-canes

Timbuck II Shopping Village (252) 453-9707

Finally have some time for yourself? This full-service salon offers all hair services and facial waxing. The kids will be excited that they also do hair wraps, braiding and airbrush tattoos in season. Walk-ins are welcome, but you can also make an appointment.

Island Tobacco

Timbuck II Shopping Village (252) 453-8163

Calling all smokers. For fine imported cigars, pipes, loose tobaccos, imported

cigarettes and clove cigarettes, this is the place for you. You'll also find dart and billiards supplies, chess sets and other gifts like Jack Daniels paraphernalia.

Joan's

Timbuck II Shopping Village (252) 453-8844

Joan's has the coolest collection of home decor that will make you feel downright covetous. You'll swoon over colorful, funky pillows, linens, lamps, prints and accessories, and the furniture is to die for. Joan's offers expert interior design services to help you pull it all together.

Just for the Beach

Timbuck II Shopping Village (252) 453-4505

Whatever you need for the beach, you'll find it here: clothing, swimwear,

sandals, towels, gear, chairs, toys, hats, sunglasses, sunscreen and more. And what would summer vacation be without fireworks and hermit crabs?

Kitty Hawk Kites

Timbuck II Shopping Village (252) 453-8845

Kitty Hawk Kites specializes in kites, toys, unique T-shirts and great Outer Banks gifts. Their recreation department boasts the world's oldest and largest hang gliding school, a kayak touring company and a kiteboarding training center.

Kitty Hawk Sports

Timbuck II Shopping Village (252) 453-4999

This water sports store offers all the beachwear you'll need to fit in with the surf and water sports crowd. Billabong, Quiksilver, Jams, Roxy, Patagonia and more brand names are top sellers. There are also souvenir Ts and sweats.

Michael's Gems and Glass

Timbuck II Shopping Village (252) 453-4310

Michael's goods are about as natural as you can get. Earth-made, sometimes man-enhanced rocks, seashells, fossils and mineral items make truly unique gifts. We like the jewelry crafted from crystals and glass and the agate geode bookends.

Miss Kitty's Old Time Photos

Timbuck II Shopping Village (252) 457-5011

This is something really fun! At Miss Kitty's you dress the whole family up in old-time costumes, from the silly to the sublime, and pose for a sepia-toned portrait. The antique-looking portraits are ready in minutes, granting immediate satisfaction and giggles. Pick out an antique-style frame to add to your portrait's allure. You can even research the history of your family surnames here. You'll be in good hands, as the folks at Miss Kitty's have won a Design Excellence award in antique photography.

Mustang Sally's

Timbuck II Shopping Village (252) 453-0892
This store offers clothing that's as fun as its name. The clothing and accessories sold here are creative and unique, perfect for the relaxed vacation lifestyle and for carrying that mood back home with you. Mustang Sally's has been a northern beaches favorite for more than 10 years. You'll find women's and juniors clothing as well as a wide range of creative gift items.

The Mystic Jewel

Timbuck II Shopping Village (252) 453-3797
The Mystic Jewel sells top quality, irresistibly unique jewelry made of sterling silver, crystal beads and semi-precious stones, including a good selection of Larimar. The owners are skilled jewelers and retailers who pride themselves on service and the fact that they hand-pick each handcrafted piece that graces their store. They honor the mystical powers of gemstones and the way they can help in shaping our bodies, minds and spirits.

Nags Head Hammocks

Timbuck II Shopping Village
          (252) 453-4611, (800) 344-6433
The Outer Banks' original hammock is now a nationally recognized brand. These famous handcrafted rope products are a must have. The shop also sells hammock

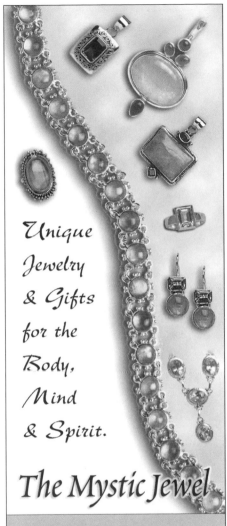

Unique
Jewelry
& Gifts
for the
Body,
Mind
& Spirit.

The Mystic Jewel

TimbuckII Shops
793 Sunset Blvd. #E.
Corolla, NC 27927
(252) 453-3797

Scarborough Lane Shoppes
1171 Duck Rd, Ste A-4
Duck, NC 27949
(252) 255-5515

or online at: themysticjewel.com

See **www.corollaguide.com** for full content, links & updates.

furniture, like rope chairs, swings, rockers, barstools and footstools. To make your hammock complete, and completely relaxing, check out the hammock accessories they have here such as pillows and hammock and swing stands. And don't miss their new all-weather furniture. Shipping is available.

Ocean Threads

Timbuck II Shopping Village` (252) 453-0888

Ocean Threads specializes in swimwear for the entire family, including maternity styles and children's suits. You'll also find accessories, flip-flops, sunglasses and the ultimate new accessory – airbrush tattoos. Brand names include Roxy, Quiksilver, Billabong, O'Neill, Rusty, Reef, Volcom and the popular Paul Frank jammies.

Ocean Treasures / Wyland and Thomas Kinkade Art Gallery and Gift Shop

Timbuck II Shopping Village` (252) 453-2383

Have you ever seen a 7-foot-tall triple dolphin sculpture? That's why this shop is called Ocean Treasures — they offer work from some of the most exacting sea life sculptors. This shop features Thomas Kinkade and Wyland artworks and gift items. You'll find paintings, sculptures, clothing, children's items, jewelry, and magnets.

Outer Banks Fudge Co.

Timbuck II Shopping Village` (252) 453-6246

Outer Banks Fudge Co. features 20 varieties of fudge and fudge-covered goodies like pretzels, graham crackers and Oreos. You'll also find Outer Banks coffee, trail mix and other snacks, cookie

See **www.corollaguide.com** for full content, links & updates.

mixes and puzzles. They can ship treats anywhere and even offer an Outer Banks care package that's all ready to go.

The Perfect Gift

Timbuck II Shopping Village` (252) 453-4330

You won't be able to leave this store without finding something for yourself or a special friend. Leather from the Brighton collection, one-of-a-kind pieces of sterling and fine jewelry, home décor items and artwork make it easy to find the perfect gift for everyone.

Sarandebity

Timbuck II Shopping Village (252) 453-6000

Sarandebity is a trendy shop with lots of personality. The huge collection of fun stuff includes fashion jewelry, collectibles, picture frames, greeting cards, kitchen and home décor items and even personalized pet collars. We like the tote bags and purses, wall sculptures and the hand-painted martini glasses (complete with drink recipe painted on the bottom of the glass).

Seaside Farm Market

Timbuck II Shopping Village (252) 453-8285

On your way in or out of Timbuck II, be sure to stop by this farm market, located right at the entrance by the stoplight. Fresh seasonal produce including sweet corn, juicy tomatoes and tree-ripened peaches will tempt you. Look for local homemade jams, sauces for seafood, local farm cheeses and fresh herbs. They stock fresh, local seafood and a full line of beers and fine wines.

Surfside Casuals

Timbuck II Shopping Village (252) 453-8834

Surfside Casuals features approximately 400 different transfer designs for T-shirts, sweatshirts, beach cover-ups and even shorts, all available in a variety of colors. They also carry pre-designed souvenir T-shirts, sweatshirts and bathing suits.

Tar Heel Trading Co.

Timbuck II Shopping Village (252) 453-3132

Tar Heel Trading Co. has been bringing American handcrafts to the Outer Banks for 27 years. Specialties include jewelry, wall sculpture and home and office décor. We especially like the puzzle boxes, kaleidoscopes and waterfowl carvings.

See **www.corollaguide.com** for full content, links & updates.

Try My Nuts Nut Company

Timbuck II Shopping Village (252) 453-4955

Gourmet nuts and yummy candies are the specialty at this shop. If you can't decide what to get, take a few of the free samples to get your taste buds working. Equally as popular as the edible treats are the souvenir hats, T-shirts, boxers and gifts.

Monteray Shores Shopping Plaza

800 block of Ocean Trail and Albacore Street, east of the stoplight

This plaza is anchored by the Food Lion grocery store and has numerous shops and eateries, plus a climbing wall that belongs to Carolina Outdoors. It's also the home of the Corolla Movies (see Recreation).

Bacchus Wine and Cheese

Monteray Plaza   (252) 453-4333

Bacchus Wine and Cheese is a specialty shop for culinary indulgence of the best kinds! They carry specialty cheeses, wines, hand-cut Angus beef and sinful desserts. You'll find real triple-cream Brie, Stilton, Manchego, Wensleydale and more than 25 other cheeses, plus gourmet crackers, fresh breads and olives. Olive oils, balsamic vinegars, specialty sauces and pastas will tempt you as well. And don't forget the wine. Bacchus has more than 750 labels from around the world and offers wine tastings to help you narrow down the selections; call for tastings reservations.

Birthday Suits

Monteray Plaza   (252) 453-4862

Birthday Suits is an Outer Banks favorite for swimwear -- in fact, it's been voted Best on the Beach for swimsuits for six years running by the Outer Banks Sentinel and Virginian-Pilot readers' polls. For kids, there's everything from swim diapers and toddler suits to board shorts to competition swimwear. Men will find surf trunks, board shorts and briefs from sizes 28 to XXX large. For women, there are mix-and-match separates, bra-sized swimwear and long-torso, maternity and mastectomy suits, all in the coolest styles. Birthday Suits carries designer and California surf brands, rash guards for kids and adults, clothing and beach-inspired accessories like sunglasses, flip-flops, hats, jewelry and purses. Love the OBX logo? You'll find all kinds of OBX accessories here.

Carolina Outdoors

Monteray Plaza   (252) 453-3685

Carolina Outdoors, a division of Kitty Hawk Kites, can set you up on the climbing wall in the courtyard or provide you with a kayak rental (see our Recreation chapter). They also sell sportswear, notably Columbia, TEVA, Royal Robbins and custom Outer Banks T-shirts and accessories. You'll also find clothing and accessories from the cheerful Life is Good brand here.

Corolla Surf Shop

Monteray Plaza   (252) 453-WAVE

The Monteray Plaza location of Corolla Surf Shop is close to everything you need: a good surf break and a great bagel shop! This location offers the same great clothing and gear as the other two shops, which are located in   Timbuck II. Their top-notch Surf School operates out of this location, offering lessons for all ages from 9 and older, and they do surf rentals and repairs here. They feature all the best brands in surf and skate clothing. Skateboarders will be happy with the newly expanded skate department selling a full line of skate equipment and accessories. See our Recreation chapter.

Dockside North Seafood Market

Monterey Plaza   (252) 453-8112

    Cooking in tonight? Stop by Dockside North, conveniently around the corner from the grocery store, for fresh fish, clams, crabmeat, soft shell crabs, scallops or oysters. They offer shrimp, crab legs and lobster steamed-to-order. The family will be happy if you bring home one of

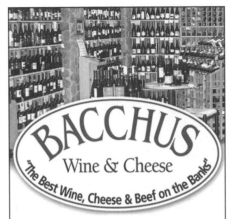

BACCHUS
Wine & Cheese
"The Best Wine, Cheese & Beef on the Banks"

4,000+ Bottles of Fine Wine
Angus Steaks · Decadent Desserts
Boar's Head Deli & Specialty Sandwiches
Domestic & Imported Cheeses
Weekly Wine Tastings

252.453.4333
Monteray Plaza, Corolla (South Side of Food Lion)

See **www.corollaguide.com** for full content, links & updates.

pottery

jewelry

Ocean Annie's

Featuring comtemporary Crafts from dozens of U.S. artisans

wood

metal-work

glass

chimes

gourmet coffee beans

Monteray Plaza   Scarborough Faire
COROLLA   DUCK
252.453.4102   252.261.3290

their Down East Clambakes to go. Beer is available here as well.

Donna Designs

Monteray Plaza   **(252) 453-0939**

Each piece of Donna Designs wearable art is hand-painted one at a time in an Outer Banks studio. You'll find top-quality women's T-shirts, pants, skirts, dresses, cotton sweaters and bags. The Ts are decorated with Donna's original designs, such as turtles, whales, flip-flops, shells or some other outdoorsy and beachy theme. Women's clothing is available in sizes small to 2x. The hand-painted kids' and babies' clothing is extremely popular. They have a big selection of straw hats and bags to suit any style and beautiful, unique Holly Yashi jewelry. You'll love the fun atmosphere in this shop.

Gray's Department Store

Monteray Plaza   **(252) 453-0852**

Here is another branch of this widespread Outer Banks department store. Gray's is one of the most popular stores on the beach for good reason. They offer the largest selection of Tommy Bahama and Fresh Produce sportswear on the Outer Banks. Gray's also has OBX gear, souvenir T-shirts, hats, cozy sweatshirts, Eliza B. sandals, belts and key chains plus sportswear for the whole family.

Just for the Beach

Monteray Plaza   **(252) 453-6106**

If you couldn't bring it or forgot it, don't worry. Just for the Beach probably has it, and they can deliver it to you before you can even miss it. Here you can rent baby equipment like cribs and strollers, cottage equipment like grills, recreational equipment like bikes, surfboards and kayaks and beach equipment like umbrellas and chairs. Just for the Beach is also a retail shop with T-shirts, swimwear, resort wear, souvenirs and hermit crabs.

Ocean Annie's

Monteray Plaza   **(252) 453-4102**

This Outer Banks gift institution features contemporary crafts from numerous artisans. Decorative and functional pottery and ceramic art is a standout here, but you'll also enjoy the wood, jewelry, metalworks, glass, chimes, frames and other gifts. Ocean Annie's also sells gourmet coffee beans, which smell so heavenly you'll have to buy a pound or two.

See **www.corollaguide.com** for full content, links & updates.

Outer Banks Books

Monteray Plaza　　　　　　(252) 457-0070

Outer Banks Books offers an incredible selection of books at extremely discounted prices — up to 60 percent off. You'll find best-selling hardbacks, paperbacks, cookbooks, special interest, fiction and literature, kids' books, self-help, regional and local titles, books on tape and CD and a lot more. Outer Banks Books also offers wireless internet access. You can use one of their computers or bring your own laptop.

Serendipity

Monteray Plaza　　　　　　(252) 453-6881

This fun little gift shop is tucked back in the courtyard, near the movie theater. Serendipity is known for unique jewelry, like the Roman glass jewelry, created from glass from the Antiquities period and set into beautiful pieces. There's sterling silver jewelry that can be monogrammed with engraving done by hand. You'll also find whimsical art here, like hand-painted wine and martini glasses, Mary Engelbreit artwork and stained glass. If you're lucky, you just might catch the owner, Julia, working on her handmade stained glass right in the shop.

Soundfeet Shoes

Monteray Plaza　　　　　　(252) 453-9787

Outer Bankers love Soundfeet because they sell the most comfortable, casual footwear for the island lifestyle. Choose from a huge selection of styles and colors in European comfort shoes and high-end brands like Birkenstock, Naot, Mephisto, Reef, Vans, Ecco, Teva and Merrell. Plus, there's a great selection of athletic shoes by New Balance, Nike, Asics, Saucony and other well-known names. This location will close at the end of 2006.

Top Nails of Corolla

Monteray Plaza　　　　　　(252) 457-0288

Your tan will look even more smashing against a perfectly rendered manicure or pedicure from Top Nails. This shop is on the back side of the shopping center next to Dockside North Seafood Market. Walk-ins are welcome, or you can call to schedule an appointment.

T-Shirt World

Monteray Plaza　　　　　　(252) 453-3133

No vacation is complete without a souvenir T-shirt to add to your collection. Here you can choose from a variety of preprinted shirts or design one of your own to be printed with decals. The whole

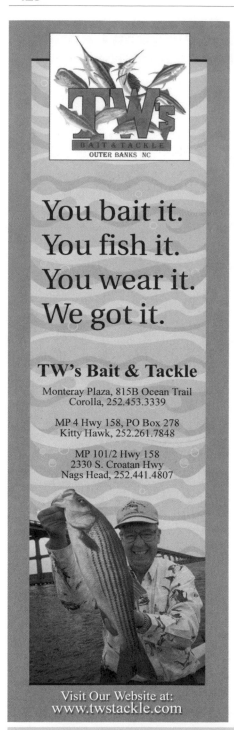

You bait it.
You fish it.
You wear it.
We got it.

TW's Bait & Tackle

Monteray Plaza, 815B Ocean Trail
Corolla, 252.453.3339

MP 4 Hwy 158, PO Box 278
Kitty Hawk, 252.261.7848

MP 101/2 Hwy 158
2330 S. Croatan Hwy
Nags Head, 252.441.4807

Visit Our Website at:
www.twstackle.com

family can get tees here with sizes from six months to XXX-large. T-Shirt World always has the most current trends in T-shirt art.

TW's Bait & Tackle

Monteray Plaza   (252) 453- 3339

There's something for everyone at TW's. Of course, TW's has all the fishing supplies you could need, but they also have a full selection of sportswear for the entire family. They carry a full line of Columbia clothing, Aftco sportswear, dresses for women and children's clothing. You'll love their T-shirts with lots of great fishing designs. They also have plenty of fun gifts and fishy home décor items. See our Recreation chapter.

Ocean Trail

The Farmer's Daughter

812 Ocean Trail, across from Monteray Plaza
(252) 453-9116

For collectibles, gifts, home décor and knickknacks galore, The Farmer's Daughter has it all and then some. Waterfowl carvings, nautical décor, garden accents, home furnishings, candles, wind chimes, art, casual apparel, jewelry, handmade crafts, flags, shell art and so much more fill this store to the gills. You can also get fudge from the Outer Banks Fudge Co.

Kitty Hawk Kites

Route 12, Ocean Trail Shopping Center
(252) 453-2904

As in their store in Timbuck II, Kitty Hawk Kites is the place to go for fun.

They have all sorts of kites, from the basic backyard variety to competition quality stunt kites. You'll also find windsocks, flags and toys.

Ace Hardware of Corolla

822 Ocean Trail   (252) 453-4441

Just north of Monteray Plaza, Ace is much more than a hardware store. Of course, they have everything you need for home maintenance and repair, including paint, tools, electrical and plumbing supplies, garden and lawn products, cleaning supplies and more. But they also sell things vacationers need, like beach chairs, hammocks, boogie boards, umbrellas, beach toys and grilling supplies. Ace also sells art supplies and home décor items.

Corolla Light Town Center

This little cluster of shops is on the corner of Ocean Trail and Austin Street, at the main entrance to Corolla Light. It's just south of the entrance to the Whalehead Club.

Back Country Outfitters

Corolla Light Town Center   (252) 453-0877

This shop is the headquarters for Kayak Corolla and the Wild Horse Safari (see Recreation). Stop by to make a reservation or inquire about these tours. The shop also sells sportswear, souvenir clothing and accessories that are perfect for wild horse fans.

Corolla Bait and Tackle

Corolla Light Town Center   (252) 453-9500

Keith Cummings of Corolla Bait and Tackle is a knowledgeable angler who loves to share his fishing tips. Stop by for bait, tackle, gear rentals, charter boat bookings and free advice. See the Recreation chapter for more information.

Dawn's Harvest Mart

Corolla Light Town Center

This fruit stand is located in the field just north of the Corolla Light Town Center. Fresh fruits like berries, peaches, plums and melons will tempt you, as will homemade breads and pies. They even carry local seafood here, like soft shells (when in season), shrimp and scallops.

Ferrari's Gourmet Market & Deli

Corolla Light Town Center   (252) 453-2555

Ferrari's is an authentic Italian deli and gourmet market. They serve a variety of hot and cold foods, like wraps and panini sandwiches made from Boar's Head meats, and Italian favorites like chicken Marsala and penne alla vodka. Enjoy a cappuccino, espresso or fresh fruit smoothie from their frozen beverage and coffee bar. Relax at one of their bistro tables, or take your order to go. Don't forget to check out the selection of gourmet items in the market, with lots of imported Italian specialties, cheeses, wine and beer. Pick up a picnic basket filled with goodies before heading to a concert on the lawn at the Whalehead Club. They also create custom gift baskets.

Island Revolution Surf Shop

Corolla Light Town Center   (252) 453-9484

Shop here for surf and skate threads, equipment and accessories. Island Revolution has a full line of surfboards, skateboards, accessories and clothing for men and women. You can check out surf videos on their plasma TVs while you shop. Purchase passes to the concrete skatepark here, and ask about the surf lessons. See our Recreation chapter for more about the Corolla Skatepark and surf lessons.

Mustang Sally's

Corolla Light Town Center   (252) 453-0554

This store offers clothing that's as fun as its name. The clothing and accessories sold here are creative and unique, perfect for the relaxed vacation lifestyle and for carrying that mood back home with you. Mustang Sally's has been a northern beaches favorite for more than 10 years. You'll find women's and juniors clothing as well as a wide range of creative gift items.

Neds Convenience Store

Corolla Light Town Center   (252) 453-8821

Neds Convenience Store stocks all sorts of snacks and grocery items, sundries and other convenience items. This is a great place to pick up last minute necessities like beer, wine and ice.

Neds Ice Cream and Sweet Treats

Corolla Light Town Center

Neds is a great stop for a cool, tasty treat. They serve hand-dipped Edy's and Bryers ice cream cones, milkshakes and a variety of sundaes. For the chocolate lover they have a variety of gourmet chocolates and old-fashioned candy. It's the perfect respite from a hot summer afternoon of shopping.

Ocean Atlantic Rentals

Corolla Light Town Center   (252) 453-2440

The original Outer Banks rental shop offers everything you need that you couldn't fit in the car. Beach equipment, baby gear, strollers, bikes and scooters, kayaks, surfboards, wetsuits, grills, rollaway beds, linens, videos and DVDs and more are available. You can reserve items online before you get here. Delivery is available.

Ocean Threads

Corolla Light Town Center   (252) 453-8967

Ocean Threads specializes in surf, swim and skate. You'll find swimwear for the entire family, including maternity styles and children's suits. You'll also find accessories, flip-flops and sunglasses, plus skateboarding gear. Brand names include

Roxy, Quiksilver, Billabong, O'Neill, Rusty, Reef, Volcom and the popular Paul Frank jammies. Looking for glow-in-the-dark body jewelry? It's here.

Old Corolla Village

Currituck Beach Lighthouse Museum Shop

Currituck Beach Lighthouse site
(252) 453-6778

The Little Light Keeper's House at the Currituck Beach Lighthouse compound is now a museum shop that will delight anyone who loves lighthouses and wild horses. It's fun to wander around in this historic building looking at the architectural elements and at the same time see every kind of lighthouse souvenir you could possibly imagine. There are T-shirts and clothing, hats, books, prints, figurines, lamps, ornaments, jewelry, magnets, patches, dishtowels, cards, postcards and more, not just for the Currituck Beach Lighthouse but for other lighthouses as well. Also for sale are wild horse clothing and memorabilia, and the profits from those items benefit the Corolla Wild Horse Fund.

The Island Bookstore

1130 Corolla Village Road   (252) 453-2292

The Island Bookstore, which also has a location in Duck, is a full-service independent bookstore with a comprehensive selection of books to please every reader. Housed in a reproduction historic building in the heart of the village, this bookseller's special

See **www.corollaguide.com** for full content, links & updates.

Bring the spirit of the garden to your home, porch and lifestyle.

LIGHTHOUSE
garden
453.0171 Historic Corolla Village

other wonderful items. Garden statuary, ironwork and architectural ornaments fill the yard and the porches.

Lightkeeper's Wife

1130-B Corolla Village Road (252) 453-4190

Sister store to Islands By Amity in Duck, The Lightkeeper's Wife is an upscale clothing boutique for hip, fashion-motivated women. You'll find trendy, fun clothing lines such as Juicy Couture, Citizens of Humanity, Free People, Three Dot, Michael Stars and Seven jeans. There's also a full line of jewelry and accessories for the contemporary, fashionable lifestyle. Look for same great store with a new name in summer '06

Old Corolla Trading Co.

1129 Schoolhouse Lane   (252) 453-9942

If you're trying to accentuate your interior decor, Old Corolla Trading Co. has a nice selection of nautical accessories and casual furniture that will bring a relaxed tone to any home. Old buoys, maritime antiques, brass nautical items, prints and local artwork are just a few of the home accents you'll find here. Old Corolla Trading Co. also sells Bauer International furniture, which features sumptuous and refined leather, mahogany and wicker pieces.

strengths include local and regional interest books, a children's section to delight every age from toddlers to teachers, and a huge selection of audio books (even on CD). New York Times bestseller hardbacks are always discounted.

Lighthouse Garden

1129 Corolla Village Road   (252) 453-0171

In a restored village home, this is one of those stores that will make you swoon. The interior itself is charming, with old doors, windows and shutters used as display stands and the original beaded board on the walls painted in old-fashioned colors. The floors creak under your feet as you wander around looking at beautiful home and porch décor such as florals and silk flowers, pillows, Guy Wolff pottery, furnishings, frames and so many

Outer Banks Style

1134 Corolla Village Road   (252) 453-4388

Outer Banks Style, housed in one of the enchanting old village homes, offers a great mix of furniture and accessories for the casual and fun Outer Banks lifestyle. You'll find local photographs and artwork, antiques, reproduction signs, pillows, rugs, lamps, linens and much more. Outer Banks

See **www.corollaguide.com** for full content, links & updates.

SPRY CREEK
Dry Goods

A Charming Display of Local and Imported Artwork
Jewelry, Handmade Soaps, Linens, Ceramics, Glassware & more

1122 COROLLA VILLAGE RD • 252.453.0199

Style is a dealer of the whimsical Brian Andreas StoryPeople books, prints and sculpture. Visit their new wine shop and pick up a bottle to enjoy during cocktail hour or to accompany a dinner at home.

Spry Creek Dry Goods

1122 Corolla Village Road   (252) 453-0199

Spry Creek is owned by lifelong Outer Banks resident Karen Whitfield and her husband, John. Karen has converted her father's old auto repair shop into a quirky, surprising shop. They kept the old bay doors and shop flooring for charm, and be sure to look for Karen's father's work bench, which came out of Penny's Hill Lifesaving Station. In the shop, Karen emphasizes local artwork like jewelry, art glass, handmade soaps and even carved decoys. She has imported linens, handcrafted ceramics from Spain, Portugal and Mexico and Mexican glassware. Spry Creek is named after a deepwater

creek just north of the shop where local fishermen used to keep their boats and a couple of local crabbers still do.

The Village Fisherman

Corolla Village Road   (252) 453-3248

The Village Fisherman is an outdoor market where you'll find whimsical gifts, local artwork and garden accessories. The shop is filled with pottery, quilts, wind chimes, candles and birdhouses. The owner, Peggy, named the shop after her husband, who is one of the last commercial fishermen in Corolla. Tote your purchases away in one of Peggy's hand-painted shopping bags.

Whalehead Club Museum Shop

Currituck Heritage Park   (252) 453-9040

Once you finish the tour at the Whalehead Club you're conveniently

The Village Fisherman
UNIQUE GIFTS

252.453.3248
Corolla Town Center & Historic Corolla Village

Diane Artware

See **www.corollaguide.com** for full content, links & updates.

Shopping Near the Old Village Center

Corolla Outback

1148 Ocean Trail   (252) 453-3452

This small stand-alone building is next to the Corolla Post Office. Corolla Outback is the place to book Corolla Outback Adventures horse tours, but it's also a great little shop that sells souvenir clothing and accessories.

Winks of Corolla

1152 Ocean Trail   (252) 453-8166

Just north of old Corolla village, Winks is a landmark store on the northern beaches. Winks sells gas, grocery items, snacks, drinks, ice, beer and wine, toiletries, sundries, local and regional books, beach needs and more. The Corolla Post Office is next door.

Big Mama's Ice Cream and Yogurt

1152 Ocean Trail   (252) 453-4960

This ice cream and frozen yogurt shop fits the bill on a hot summer day when you're in need of a tasty treat. Next to Winks and the post office, it's conveniently located near the local attractions.

poised to do a little souvenir hunting in the Museum Shop. In one of the rooms of the historic home, the shop offers items that have significance pertaining to the home. For instance, during the restoration the original copper roof had to be replaced. The old roof shingles with a perfect green patina were given to artists, who made them into jewelry, picture frames, lamps and special ornaments with a new design each year. The shop also sells bath salts in honor of Mrs. Knight, who liked to take seawater baths. You'll also find books, postcards, miniature decoys and special edition T-shirts, hats and sweatshirts. There are beautiful photographs and posters, even a wooden replica of the Whalehead Club.

COROLLA RESTAURANTS 🐎

Choosing where to dine in Corolla is an enviable task. Discriminating vacationers demand top-quality dining, and Corolla restaurants have stepped up to serve them well. Whether you're looking for breakfast, lunch or dinner, fast fare or intimate dining, you'll find it here.

There are three fast-food chains in Corolla, but all of the other restaurants are locally owned, allowing for creativity and individuality you'll never be able to find at a chain.

Seafood is the main event in almost every local restaurant because that's what is the freshest and that's what everybody wants. Tuna, mahi mahi, rockfish, flounder and a variety of other fish, plus blue crabs, clams, shrimp, scallops, mussels and oysters are the most popular local catches. If you're here in early summer, don't miss a chance to taste the regional delicacy of fresh soft-shell crabs. Of course, local chefs also serve meats, pasta, vegetarian offerings and fresh local produce. Mainland Currituck County is home to many farms, so fresh vegetables are available year round.

Restaurants in Corolla are able to serve liquor in addition to beer and wine, so expect to find a full bar in many establishments. In the height of summer, local restaurants can be quite crowded. This is a testament to their quality, but it's also a sign that you need to make reservations. You should know, too, that dining out in extremely large parties can be taxing to some restaurants, while others can handle it with ease. If you must dine out en masse, always call ahead to make sure your restaurant of choice can accommodate a large party (and to give them a warning that you're coming).

Dining is casual here, even in the finest restaurants. Dressing up means putting on long pants (or nice shorts) and a collared shirt or a sundress. Most Corolla restaurants close for at least part of the winter and early spring, though a few stay open year round. Call ahead if you're visiting in the off-season.

Pine Island Diner

N.C. Highway 12, next to Hampton Inn
(252) 453-4828

Pine Island Diner brings sit-down, kid-friendly dining to the Pine Island area.

The atmosphere is reminiscent of a 1950s diner, with checkerboard floors and booth or bar-stool seating. Expect diner-type fare, like burgers, sandwiches, fries, milk shakes, malts and sundaes. A welcome surprise is a pizza oven. Beer and wine are available. Pine Island Diner is open for lunch and dinner.

The Pizza Guy

501 Old Stoney Road, Pine Island

(252) 453-9976

Those staying in Pine Island will be glad to see The Pizza Guy. This is the only restaurant right at Pine Island, with a location just north of the water tower. Pizzas, subs and appetizers like bread sticks, salads, mozzarella sticks and more are available. You can eat in, take out or call for free delivery. The Pizza Guy offers delivery from the Duck Research Pier to Ocean Hill.

Bunkers Grille and Bar at The Currituck Club

620 Currituck Clubhouse Drive

(252) 453-0926

Whether or not you're golfing, make time for a meal at Bunkers, inside the beautiful clubhouse on the spectacular Currituck Club grounds. Bunkers offers lunch daily, with chef specials and house-made soups. The menu features a variety of appetizers, salads and sandwiches. Full bar service is available. Bunkers is open year round, every day but Thanksgiving and Christmas.

Ocean Club Centre at the Currituck Club

GiGi's

520 G Old Stoney Road   (252) 453-2929

Gigi's is a little taste of Italy on the Outer Banks! This restaurant has a menu that boasts a sampling of Italy, with the chef's own family recipes. He's even named the place after his grandmother Gigi, whose cooking is his inspiration. The homemade cannolis are delicious! As you dine, beautiful murals of Italian landscapes hand-painted by local artist Elizabeth Kays surround you. There is no separate kid's menu, but the chef can accommodate the little ones with smaller portions. Gigi's is open year round for dinner only. Reservations are recommended, especially in season.

Metropolis

Ocean Club Centre   (252) 453-6167

Metropolis is a great spot for an evening out at the beach if you want something different from a grill and bar atmosphere. This contemporary tapas and martini bar offers an environment as urban and chic as the name suggests. The chef describes the menu as American fusion, and they borrow exotic flavors of Asia. Metropolis has an extensive beer, wine and liquor menu. They're open until 2 a.m. and don't have booster seats or a kid's menu.

Monteray Plaza

Bacchus Wine & Cheese

Monteray Plaza   (252) 453-4333

Baccus is located on the south end of the plaza and offers wine, cheese and gourmet-foods. It's also a great deli. You can get fantastic deli sandwiches, subs, wraps and salads for take-out or to eat in. Sandwiches are made with Boar's Head meats and domestic and imported cheeses, and there are yummy gourmet side items and sinful desserts to accompany them. It's open every day in season. Ask about the weekly wine tastings and catering services. See our Shopping chapter for more about the wine and gourmet foods.

Beach Sweets and Treats

Monteray Plaza   (252) 453-6999

Tucked back in the courtyard at Monteray Plaza, near the movie theater, this sweet shop offers hand-dipped ice cream, candy and homemade fudge. You can also get coffee drinks, including espresso and cappuccino, perfect for a

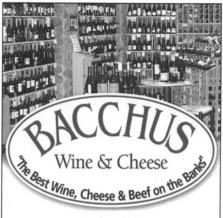

pick-me-up when you're out shopping. Grab some beach reading from their selection of newspapers and magazines.

China King

Monteray Plaza   (252) 457-0158

China King offers all the Chinese favorites in a bright, clean atmosphere. Order at the counter or partake of the popular daily buffet. China King is perfect for take-out for large crowds.

Whalehead Pizza and Corolla Brew Pub

Monteray Plaza   (252) 453-6638

Stop here for gourmet pizza that you can eat in, take out or have delivered for free. The Brew Pub has local Outer Banks Brewing Station beers on tap and a variety of other beers as well, including seasonal brews. The pub menu features sandwiches, hot dogs, German sausages and burgers. Try the triple-decker club; like the menu says, "you can see Virginia from atop of it." They have a full dinner menu with seafood entrees and some German specialties that pair nicely with the brew. It's open for lunch and dinner and is in the courtyard area next to the movie theater.

Dairy Queen

Monteray Plaza   (252) 453-3130

You probably know what to expect from this national chain: soft-serve ice cream, served in cones, cups, shakes, sundaes and a variety of creative concoctions. You can also get hot dogs and other quick food, plus delicious ice cream cakes.

Dr. Unks Bar

Monteray Plaza   (252) 453-0053

Dr. Unks Bar is a fun, new Corolla nightspot. Located in the same building as Tomato Patch Pizzeria, Dr. Unks serves a late-night menu. They have a fully stocked bar and feature live music during the summer season -- call ahead for a schedule.

La Fogata Mexican Restaurant

Monteray Plaza   (252) 453-9717

The three La Fogata Restaurants, one in Nags Head, one in Kitty Hawk and this one in Corolla, are locals' favorites for inexpensive, delicious meals. The exhaustive menu of authentic Mexican specialties is a little overwhelming, but complimentary warm chips and spicy salsa hold you over while you decide.

Lighthouse Bagels

Monteray Plaza   (252) 453-9998

Start the day at Lighthouse Bagels with fresh-brewed coffee and fresh baked bagels, pastries and muffins. You can also order fresh-cooked eggs and meats. Bread is baked here daily, and in the summer, Krispy Kreme doughnuts are brought in. Later in the day, they serve bagel or grilled sandwiches or subs with Boar's Head meats. Lighthouse Bagels is open for breakfast and lunch in season.

North Beach Bistro

Monteray Plaza   (252) 453-0788

This little bistro-style restaurant offers lunch and dinner every day in season. At lunch, choose from a variety of sandwiches, wraps and salads. They serve classic seafood specialties, steaks, pasta and vegetarian dishes and chef's specials every night. A full kids' menu is available. Save room for the gourmet desserts, and linger over a latte or cappuccino. Beer, wine and mixed drinks are offered. Reservations are recommended in season. North Beach Bistro also offers full-service catering.

Outer Banks Coffee Company

Monteray Plaza   (252) 453-0200

The sunny-orange atmosphere in the coffee shop is enough to wake you up, but you'll want to try the coffee too — they have quite a variety and it's roasted in the shop to delight your olfactory senses. All the usual coffee drinks are offered, as are tea and homemade pastries and other sweets, all baked in the Coffee Company's bakery. Get connected here with the free wireless Internet access. Stop by the mini-newsstand on the corner to get your a.m.

paper and you're all set to go.

Philly Steak Subs

Monteray Plaza   (252) 453-4239

You don't find many authentic Philadelphia cheesesteaks in these parts, but this is the real thing. Philly Steak Subs uses marinated lean steak, chipped on the grill and served on a split-top Amoroso roll imported from Philadelphia. You can choose from several varieties of cheesesteaks or try an oven-baked sub or burger. Definitely try the French fries or onion rings and put a quarter in the jukebox.

Smokey's Restaurant

Monteray Plaza   (252) 453-4050

This Corolla original is a family-style restaurant that will please everyone. Its specialties include house-made North Carolina barbecue, baby-back ribs, burgers, Southern fried chicken, yellow fin tuna, fried and steamed shrimp and crab cakes. The side dishes, such as cole slaw, baked beans and onion rings, are the best. Many items are available for take out. It's open for lunch and dinner. Reservations are not accepted.

Striper's Bar and Grill

Monteray Plaza   (252) 453-4345

The creative chefs at Striper's whip up daily specials and serve all the favorites — seafood, steaks, burgers and chicken. We like the rockfish. They have steamed seafood specials from 3 p.m. to 5 p.m. every day. Striper's is open for lunch and dinner every day and offers live entertainment. Call ahead for a schedule. A kid's menu is available.

Subway

Monteray Plaza   (252) 457-1080

It is presumed that you know all the attributes of Subway, with its nationally recognized made-to-order subs, wraps and salads. The Corolla location is conveniently located in the Monteray Plaza shopping center. Subway is perfect for fueling up during a busy day of shopping, or ordering lunch to go for a picnic on the beach.

Sundogs Sports Bar and Grill

Monteray Plaza   (252) 453-GAME (4263)

For lunch and dinner, this is a great family-friendly restaurant. The grill offers an array of appetizers along with steamed seafood, sandwiches, burgers, po' boys and hot dogs plus full entrees like seafood and ribs. A children's menu is available.

See **www.corollaguide.com** for full content, links & updates.

Looking for a little action in quiet Corolla? Sundogs is also a late-night sports bar with TVs, a pool table, trivia games and a fully stocked bar where you can hang out and shoot the breeze. In the summer, Sundogs features karaoke and live entertainment on weeknights (no one under age 21 is allowed after 10 p.m.).

Tomato Patch Pizzeria

Monteray Plaza   **(252) 453-4500**

A longtime Corolla favorite, Tomato Patch offers gourmet pizzas with a variety of standard and more unusual toppings (like salami, gyro meat, caramelized onion or grilled eggplant). Tomato Patch also serves calzones, classic pasta dishes, fresh garden salads and seafood baskets, including po' boys and fish and chips. It's open for lunch, dinner and even late night. They have a fully stocked bar named Dr. Unks (see the writeup in this section).

Timbuck II Shopping Village

Big Buck's Ice Cream

Timbuck II Shopping Village (252) 453-3188

When all that shopping starts to wear you down, head to Big Buck's Ice Cream in the West building for a treat. Choose from more than 50 flavors of ice cream, sherbet, sorbet, yogurt, soft serve and frozen custard. You can get any flavor made into a shake, split, sundae or float, even a brownie sundae — yum! They have an espresso bar for a real pick-me-up. Candies, homemade chocolates and taffy are also available. Check out the Big Buck's T's.

See **www.corollaguide.com** for full content, links & updates.

Giant Slice Pizza

Timbuck II Shopping Village (252) 453-3199

Giant Slice Pizza has been a Corolla favorite for more than 12 years. Located in the South building at Timbuck II, Giant Slice bakes hand-tossed New York-style pizza with your choice of more than 18 toppings. The pies are baked to perfection in their stone ovens. Other popular choices are their appetizers, stromboli, calzones, baked wings and Italian desserts. This pizza restaurant is for carry out or delivery only. They offer free delivery from Pine Island through Ocean Hill and can accommodate any large orders.

Grouper's Grille and Wine Bar

Timbuck II Shopping Village (252) 453-4077

Grouper's, in the East building, is a Corolla favorite that's been pleasing diners since 1996. The menu offers Angus beef, lean-generation pork, local and international seafood, pasta, vegetarian entrees, creative salads and house-made desserts, all prepared with distinctive flair. Grouper's wine list is extensive and offers a large by-the-glass selection. The restaurant has even won the Wine Spectator award seven years in a row! The atmosphere is upscale but casual and is entirely smoke-free. Reservations are recommended.

Guava Jelly's

Timbuck II Shopping Village (252) 453-6777

This is a place to sit back and be happy. The name Guava Jelly's was taken from a Bob Marley song, and that sets the light and mellow tone for the atmosphere and staff. The owner strives to serve inexpensive, healthy, quick meals without a lot of drama. Breakfast is perfect,

See **www.corollaguide.com** for full content, links & updates.

with no surprises, and lunch and dinner feature California-influenced wraps and sandwiches. A kids' menu is available. Sit inside or out on the deck and enjoy the reggae music, which will be live at times.

Mike Dianna's Grill Room

Timbuck II Shopping Village (252) 453-4336

Mike Dianna's Grill Room is quickly becoming a legendary Outer Banks restaurant. It is most well known for its excellently prepared meats — USDA Prime beef, baby back ribs, lamb, chicken and veal — cooked over a mesquite grill. Seafood is treated just as beautifully, and there are daily pasta specials. The distinctive wine selection won Wine Spectator's Award of Excellence in 2005. This is a fine-dining but casual establishment, with a soundfront view. They have a new outdoor deck and bar

where you can enjoy live music in season. Open for dinner only, the restaurant is kid-friendly and offers a kids' menu. Mike Dianna's Grill Room also offers on- and off-site catering. Reservations are requested for groups of seven or more.

North Banks Restaurant & Raw Bar

Timbuck II Shopping Village (252) 453-3344

North Banks, in the West building, is contemporary and high-energy in a refined sort of way. Filet mignon and lobster are the house specialties. They also have several preparations of local fish every night and a raw bar offering up the freshest local delicacies. It's open for lunch and dinner and has a fully stocked bar featuring daily drink specials. This is a smaller restaurant with only about 50 seats,

See **www.corollaguide.com** for full content, links & updates.

and reservations are not accepted. Take-out is available here.

Route 12 Steak and Seafood

Timbuck II Shopping Village (252) 453-4644

Route 12 has a casual, quasi-roadhouse atmosphere that's appealing for the whole family. You can get local seafood, choice grade beef, duck, pasta dishes and ribs. A few of their "must try" selections are the crab bisque and the Ahi tuna pepper filet. The chef is a veteran of many Outer Banks kitchens and has quite a local following. Route 12 is open for lunch and dinner, with daily specials and a full ABC license. Kids are welcome with a menu of their own. It's located immediately south of the main Timbuck II complex, next to Brew Thru and the video store. Call ahead for reservations, especially in the busy summer months.

Sooey's BBQ and Rib Shack

Timbuck II Shopping Village (252) 453-4423

Sooey's serves up authentic Eastern NC barbecue and ribs. You can also dine on fried chicken or burgers. They have a kids' menu. You can sit inside or out or get everything to go. They're open for lunch and dinner and serve beer and wine. Sooey's has a Nags Head location across from Jockey's Ridge.

Steamers Shellfish To Go

Timbuck II Shopping Village (252) 453-3305

Steamers comes to the rescue of Corolla vacationers who want to eat in but don't want to cook. This establishment offers a variety of entrees, kids' meals, local seafood, soups, salads, side dishes and desserts for take-out. All you do is order

See **www.corollaguide.com** for full content, links & updates.

*This ocean scene can be viewed in person behind the
Tomato Patch restaurant in Monterey Plaza.*

by phone and then pick it up and bring it home. They steam the seafood for you, and there's a waterfront deck with picnic tables if you decide you just can't wait until you get home! The most popular item here is the Steamer Pot To Go, packed with your choice of shellfish, corn on the cob, red potatoes, onions and all the necessary complements, including claw crackers, butter, cocktail sauce and lemons. You can take it home to steam yourself. Steamers is on the soundside of Timbuck II.

Corolla Light Town Center

Cosmo's Pizza

Corolla Light Town Center   (252) 453-4666

Pizza is the perfect vacation food, especially when you're feeding a crowd. Cosmo's pies are a special treat, with perfectly soft and chewy crust and an abundance of toppings. They also serve up fresh-made subs and salads. You can dine in or take out at this location. Cosmos is open for lunch and dinner.

Nicoletta's Italian Café

Corolla Light Town Center   (252) 453-4004

Nicoletta's offers exquisite preparations of Italian classics and puts a creative Italian spin on local ingredients like fresh seafood. The menu changes frequently so you can return again and again for new surprises. This is one of the finer restaurants in Corolla, with an intimate atmosphere and award-winning wine list. It's open for dinner only. Reservations are requested.

Northern Light Pastries and Coffee

Corolla Light Town Center   (252) 453- 0201

Northern Light Pastries and Coffee lures customers with the heavenly smells of freshly prepared baked goods. In the morning, try doughnuts, sticky buns, muffins and fresh-roasted coffee. You'll want to stop here for fresh-baked breads. For special treats, try the pastries, cookies and cakes. Cakes can be baked and beautifully decorated to order. Pick up your morning newspaper here.

See **www.corollaguide.com** for full content, links & updates.

Classic Italian Cuisine

Serving Dinner Nightly

Reservations Recommended

Nicoletta's Italian Cafe

COROLLA LIGHT TOWN CENTER • 252-453-4004

The Wild Horse Café

Corolla Light Town Center

(252) 453-8463

The Wild Horse Café is open for breakfast, lunch and dinner every day in season. The family-friendly restaurant is an American Grill. Choose from a variety of sandwiches, wraps and burgers for lunch. For dinner, feast on steaks and fresh seafood dishes. Large parties can be accommodated.

In or Near the Old Village Center

Corolla Pizza and Deli

Austin Complex, 1152 Ocean Trail

(252) 453-8592

A longtime locals' favorite, Corolla Pizza and Deli is a take-out restaurant offering New York style pizza by the pie or

This shady spot beside Corolla Village Bar-B-Que is the site of many a summer picnic.

See **www.corollaguide.com** for full content, links & updates.

WHY COOK TONIGHT? CALL 457-0076 FOR TAKE-OUT

COROLLA VILLAGE BAR-B-QUE

North Carolina BBQ, Ribs and BBQ Chicken!

slice. They also serve up delicious hot and cold subs, sandwiches, Philly cheesesteaks and more. They offer free delivery after 5 p.m.; call for details. Open almost all year round for lunch and dinner, they can handle large orders with ease, so feeding the entire (extended) family is no problem!

Corolla Village Barbecue

1129 Corolla Village Road   (252) 457-0076

Locals sing the praises of the Carolina pork barbecue sandwiches served at this little restaurant that sits in the heart of old Corolla village. At meal times, the delicious smell of barbecuing pork, ribs and chicken lures customers from all over the village. This is a carry-out restaurant only, but there are a few picnic tables close by. You can also get soft-serve ice cream here, the perfect treat on a hot summer day. It's open for lunch and dinner, until 8 p.m., in season. 🐎

COROLLA ACCOMMODATIONS

ost vacationers at Corolla rent a private home for their vacation accommodations.

As you'll see below, there are only two hotels in the area, together offering only 166 hotel rooms. Meanwhile, there are more than 5,000 rental homes on the Currituck Outer Banks.

Most of Corolla's visitors — up to 50,000 people a week in the summer — rent a home. Almost all of the homes are relatively new and offer a wide range of amenities. The majority of the homes are larger than 5,000 square feet and offer pools and hot tubs; some even have home gyms and fitness centers. Since such large homes are readily available, many of them are rented for weddings (usually requiring a special contract), family reunions, corporate retreats or other gatherings. The trend in Corolla vacationing is for several families to rent a large home together, splitting the cost of the house and all staying under one roof. Some families prefer to rent neighboring homes. See the Vacation Rentals section below for more about renting a home.

Hotels

Hampton Inn and Suites Outer Banks Corolla

333 Audubon Drive, N.C. Highway 12, Pine Island   (252) 453-6565

This hotel is on the oceanfront at Pine Island, halfway between Duck and Corolla, which are both about 7 miles away. The grand-looking hotel has 123 rooms, both standard and larger studio suites, more than half of them with an ocean view. Every room has a balcony or patio, a sleeper sofa, microwave, refrigerator, coffeemaker, ironing equipment and hair dryer. Rooms have either one king-size bed or two queens. Their special on-the-house breakfast is included with the room rate. For recreation, Hampton Inn offers beach access, chair and umbrella rental (in season), five pools (an indoor pool and hot tub, an outdoor pool, an outdoor kids' pool and a lazy river), a game room and a fitness center. The Pine Island Racquet Club is just across the street, and anyone can reserve a tennis or squash court for a

fee. Conference and meeting rooms are available here. Call for rate availability. The hotel is open year round.

Inn at Corolla Light

1066 Ocean Trail

(252) 453-3340, (800) 215-0772

Located on the sound side in the Corolla Light resort, the Inn at Corolla Light is all about pampering its guests. Rooms are furnished with king- or queen-size beds, all with pillow-top mattresses, and sleep from two to four people. Many rooms have kitchenettes, whirlpool tubs, fireplaces or sleeper sofas. The inn actually hovers over Currituck Sound, so the views from the back rooms are amazing. Guests also have access to a video library, bicycles or, at an added cost, Jet Skis and horse tours. A pool and stone hot tub and a 400-

See **www.corollaguide.com** for

OLE PICTURE

ocated 3/10 of a mile north of the Currituck Beach Lighthouse.

foot pier and gazebo are on the property, and guests have access to all of the numerous Corolla Light amenities, which include five pools, beach access, tennis courts, the sports center, nature trails and planned activities for kids in the summer.

To truly pamper yourself, ask about the inn's spa packages available at the Spa at Corolla (see our Recreation chapter), located about seven minutes from the inn. The inn is open year round, and rates range from $169 to $325 in the summer season ($85-$215 in the wintertime). Packages and specials are available year round. There is not a restaurant on site, but several restaurants are nearby and a continental-plus breakfast is offered to guests every morning.

Vacation Rentals

Corolla is a vacation rental destination. Rental fees depend primarily upon proximity to the water and size of the home. For instance, a four- or five-bedroom home, mid-island, might run anywhere from $1,500 to $3,000 a week, while an eight-bedroom, oceanfront home could cost $10,000 a week or more. A four-bedroom soundfront home would probably be around $2,500 to $4,000 a week. Every rental company has extensive rental brochures and websites that highlight each property with all its amenities and price ranges. Summer rates are obviously the most expensive, while fall and spring are less expensive and winter is the least expensive of all. Most homes do not allow pets, but some do, so call around if it's important to you.

See **www.corollaguide.com** for full content, links & updates.

Many of the rental homes are in amenity-laden subdivisions that have community swimming pools, hot tubs, tennis courts and bike paths for their guests to use. Ask your rental agent about such communities. One of the largest is Corolla Light, which has several pools, a sports and fitness center, fitness classes, activities for kids and families and much more.

Check our Real Estate section online at www.corollaguide.com for information on vacation home sales and builders.

Atlantic Realty

Timbuck II Shopping Village (252) 453-4110

Atlantic Realty manages 250 properties from Corolla to South Nags Head. The properties range from one to eight bedrooms, oceanfront to soundfront, and many include access to private or community pools and tennis courts. Some

properties are dog friendly. Seasonal and year-round
rentals are available. Because this is a smaller company, you'll be guaranteed personable service. It's next to Kitty Hawk Kites in the Timbuck II Shopping Village.

Brindley Beach Vacations

Whalehead Bay Shoppes

(252) 453-3335, (877) 642-3224

Brindley Beach Vacations offers 150+ properties in the Corolla area and specialize in personalized service. They have properties in a variety of price ranges, from four- to eight-bedroom homes, and most have pools and access to community amenities. Some homes are pet friendly. They offer concierge services, and upon check-in you'll receive a complimentary beach bag and two passes to the new Corolla Skatepark.Carolina Designs Realty

Carolina Designs Realty

1197 Duck Road

(252) 261-3934, (800) 368-3825

Carolina Designs manages more than 300 premium rental homes from Corolla to South Nags Head and takes pride in the superior quality of service provided to both guests and owners. Most of the vacation homes have a swimming pool and a hot tub and many have access to community pools and tennis courts. Most homes are equipped with wireless internet access.

Corolla Classic Vacations

1196 Ocean Trail

(252) 453-9660, (866) 453-9660

Corolla Classic Vacations offers 200 properties in the Corolla area. Properties range from four to 10 bedrooms, and most of them are very close to the beach. This hands-on company strives to rent only well-maintained, top-of-the-line homes. Most homes have private pools, and some have access to community amenities. Some pet friendly rentals are available.

Élan Vacations

8624 Caratoke Highway, Powells Point

(252) 491-8787, (866) 760-3526

Élan represents approximately 90 homes in the Corolla area, with an additional 40 homes in the southern beaches. With a quality over quantity approach to property management, the company represents homes that vary in size and location, and all are well

Photo courtesy: Seaside Vacations

Vacation rentals in the four-wheel-drive areas north of Corolla offer seclusion, beautiful beaches and a chance to get away with your crew.

See **www.corollaguide.com** for full content, links & updates.

maintained and amenity rich. They have a standard early arrivals program and daily newspaper delivery for all guests from Memorial to Labor Day. Upon check-in you'll receive a welcome basket that includes the best of local products and beach essentials. They even include a guidebook to Corolla.

Karichele Realty

Timbuck II Shopping Village
         (252) 453-2377, (800) 453-2377
Karichele offers about 175 properties in the Corolla area, a great many of them in the isolated off-road area north of Corolla. Properties range in size from two to nine bedrooms. Some homes offer private pools and hot tubs. Want to bring along the family pet? They offer some pet friendly rentals. This is a small, family-owned business that offers personal service.

Kitty Dunes Rentals

111-C Corolla Light Village Shops
         (252) 453-3863, (877) 453-3863
Kitty Dunes has about 200 properties in the Corolla area, including a few in the four-wheel-drive territory. Most of the homes have private pools, and many oceanfront homes have walkways right to the beach. Specializing in Outer Banks vacations for more than 30 years, Kitty Dunes caters to all vacationers with ocean-to-sound properties in all price ranges.

Beach Realty & Construction/ Kitty Hawk Rentals

807 H Ocean Trail
         (252) 453-4141, (800) 635-1559
Beach Realty & Construction/Kitty Hawk Rentals manages more than 400

See **www.corollaguide.com** for full content, links & updates.

vacation homes from Ocean Hill to South Nags Head. Many of the homes have multiple master suites, pools, hot tubs and rec rooms, complete with pool tables. They are committed to offering exceptional homes and great service.

Prudential Resort Realty

Timbuck II Shopping Village
(252) 453-8700, (800) 458-3830

Prudential Resort Realty handles approximately 160 properties in the Corolla area, from Ocean Sands to Ocean Hill and everywhere in between. They offer a wide range of homes, from two to nine bedrooms, many with private swimming pools. The friendly staff at Resort Realty can meet anyone's needs with homes in all price ranges.

Photo courtesy: Seaside Vacations

Many rentals come with access to amenities such as the gym at the Currituck Club.

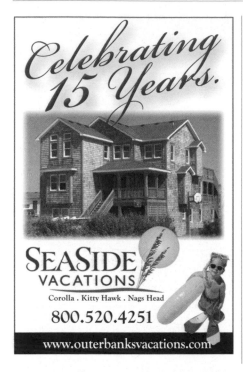

ResortQuest Outer Banks

1023 Ocean Trail
(252) 453-3033, (800) 962-0201
ResortQuest represents 400 properties in the Corolla area, so if you're looking for something very specific, they're bound to have it. A wide range of homes is available, from large to small, ocean to sound and everything in between. They offer many homes that are perfect for hosting special events and weddings and even have an event coordinator on staff. The office is directly across from the Corolla Light Sports Center.

Seaside Vacations

Whalehead Bay Shoppes
(252) 453-8030, (888) 267-6552
Seaside Vacations is celebrating 15 years of providing vacation home rentals on the

A postcard of Corolla from the 1970s. If we had only bought property then!

See **www.corollaguide.com** for full content, links & updates.

Outer Banks, so their good reputation is well established. A mid-sized company, Seaside offers more than 300 properties from Carova Beach to South Nags Head. A range of amenity-laden properties is available in Corolla and the four-wheel-drive area. They are mostly four to eight bedrooms, with many on the oceanfront.

Shoreline Preferred Properties
Ocean Club Centre at the Currituck Club
(800) 449-2036

Shoreline Preferred Properties manages 50 properties from Corolla to South Nags Head and is committed to offering personalized service. They specialize in superior vacation homes with upscale décor and modern amenities. Homes range in size from four to10 bedrooms, and most have private pools and hot tubs. Hosting a special event on the Outer Banks? Shoreline offers event planning. The office is located on Old Stoney Road.

Southern Shores Realty
5 Ocean Boulevard, Southern Shores
(252) 261-2000, (800) 334-1000

Southern Shores Realty offers about 50 homes in the Corolla area. A wide variety of properties is available, from four to eight bedrooms, and most of the rental homes have swimming pools. This established and trusted company has been serving the Outer Banks since 1947.

Stan White Realty & Construction
812 Ocean Trail
(252) 453-6131, (800) 753-6200

Stan White offers well over 100 properties in the Corolla area, from ocean

See **www.corollaguide.com** for

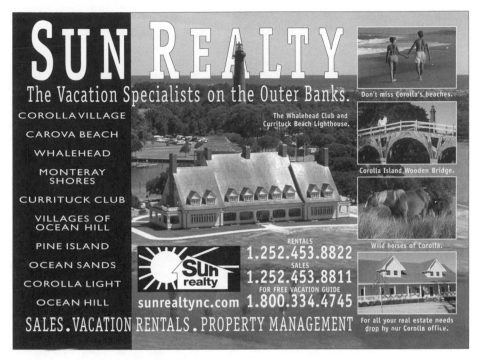
to sound. The properties encompass a range of sizes and amenities. Some pet-friendly homes are available. Want to take a last-minute vacation? Stan White offers short-term reservations on some properties. The staff is proud of its personal touch and guarantees that a real live person will always answer the phones during business hours.

Sun Realty

1135 Ocean Trail

(252) 453-8822, (800) 334-4745

Sun Realty is the largest vacation rental company on the Outer Banks and covers the Corolla area, including some beautiful homes in the off-road area. Sun has numerous homes from the ocean to the sound, ranging from two to 10 bedrooms

as well as condominiums. Weekly and weekend rentals are available. They also offer concierge services for weddings and reunions. This company has been handling Outer Banks real estate for 26 years.

Twiddy & Company Realtors

1127A Schoolhouse Lane

(252) 457-1100, (800) 489-4339

Twiddy & Company has been helping vacationing families and friends find their ideal vacation home since 1978. Twiddy offers more than 725 homes in Duck, Corolla and the four-wheel-drive beaches, scattered from the ocean to the Currituck Sound. The selection of homes is wide and varied, so you're sure to find the home that's perfect for you.

See **www.corollaguide.com** for full content, links & updates.

Village Realty

501 Hunt Club Drive

(252) 453-9650; (877) 546-5362

Village Realty represents about 250 properties in the Corolla area and manages homes in the Currituck Club. They offer homes from the ocean to the golf course, ones with pools, elevators, even pet-friendly homes. Village Realty has rentals to accommodate special events, including several in the Currituck Club that are specially equipped for weddings and catered affairs. The office is within 3 miles of most all the properties. 🐎

See **www.corollaguide.com** for full content, links & updates.